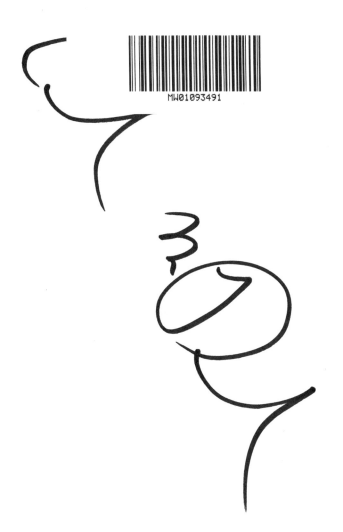

The events and conversations in this book have been set
down to the best of the authors ability, although some
names and details have been changed to protect the
privacy of individuals.

First Edition: July 2020

Cover and interior design by Olivier Darbonville

ISBN 978-0-578-70897-3 (paperback)

Published by Leader 193, LLC
www.leader193.com

LEADER 193

THE PROCESS, ART, AND SCIENCE OF LEADERSHIP

*How Leaders Inspire
Confidence and Clarity in
Combat, in the Boardroom,
and at the Kitchen Table*

ERROL DOEBLER

CONTENTS

INTRODUCTION

ROGER WAS CLEARLY FRUSTRATED. "NO PROJECT EVER seems to get fully completed. All we do is move from one fire to the next. Everyone is so stressed out that they've become lethargic and unmotivated. I'm not even sure sometimes what they are working on. My boss, and everyone else for that matter, is constantly on my ass to fix what is important to them. It's all becoming untenable."

This is how Roger, the Chief Technology Officer of a services company that runs entirely off the platform he is responsible for building and maintaining, summarized his current situation.

"So, what do you do about it?" I asked.

"What do you mean?" He replied.

"I mean, what do you do about everything you just described?" I asked again.

Roger paused and thought about my question for a moment. Then he provided me the set of nondescript, non-specific answers I've become so accustomed to hearing as I begin working with new clients. "I just get it done. I crack the whip. We come together and work for however long it takes to finish the job."

"Can you be more specific?" I asked.

"I just told you what I do," he responded with a tinge of defensiveness.

"You told me you crack the whip. What does that mean?"

Roger paused again to think. He is very mild-mannered, but I could feel he was not comfortable answering these very basic questions. "You don't know what I mean by 'crack the whip'?"

It was important for me to tread lightly because my intention was not to put Roger on the defensive, but more questions needed to be asked for him to see some things for himself.

"I think I do," I responded. "Let's change gears just a bit. How do you feel when those things are happening? How do you feel when you and your team don't complete projects or are constantly putting out fires? How do you feel when everyone is on your ass?"

"What do you mean?" he replied again to my new inquiry.

"I mean, how does that all make you feel? What emotions are you feeling when those things happen?" I asked in anticipation for a familiar response at the mention of the word "emotion."

"Errol, I'm not an emotional person. I just get it done. I told you that it is stressful and untenable." Roger replied as he unconsciously rubbed his face and tapped his pencil on the table. Even though we were on a remote video call, I could feel his energy. It was a little uncomfortable, but I needed Roger to go there with me.

I continued to gently ask Roger questions around how he felt and the things he did. He acknowledged that stress wasn't exactly an emotion, but the result of one—or many—negative emotions. We were beginning to get somewhere. Roger then acknowledged that, yes, he had emotions. He just didn't express them in an overly dramatic way.

Roger shared that he couldn't describe in detail the things he did in response to his emotions or current situation at work. "It's just intuition, Errol. I've been doing it for so long I can't really describe it. I just act and it gets done." But, not done in nearly the fashion or with the results he would like, he explained. Roger's negative energy was coming down a bit.

As we slowly turned the conversation to him and away from his external environment, Roger began to truly consider my questions. We put to the side for a moment what Roger did and focused on how he felt. "I guess I feel frustrated," he said.

"Why do you feel frustrated?" I asked.

"Well, I guess because I want to do a good job and it just doesn't feel like I'm doing a good job."

"And how does that make you feel?"

This time the answers came more quickly. "Like I shouldn't be in charge. Like I'm not worthy of my position. Like I'm not good enough to do this."

"And how does that make you feel?" I asked again.

Roger didn't have to search for this answer. "Scared."

And so began our working relationship, in which Roger would learn a new way to lead.

This is how most of my clients feel when they start working

with me. They know they need to change the way they lead, but they don't know what to do. Worse yet, the stakes are so high that they feel fear at the prospect of making the wrong move. The leaders I work with experience an incredible amount of pressure to perform, and yet they don't feel in control of the teams that are supposed to help them get to the finish line. They feel frustrated because their instincts on how to handle the stressful situations they encounter are not serving them well. They feel afraid because they are stuck in their current leadership behavior and have no idea how to do things differently. They feel afraid because they realize they would rather continue behaving in a way that is familiar to them, despite its ineffectiveness, rather than try a new behavior. Ultimately the frustration, uncertainty, and fear lead to helplessness.

Because I'm no stranger to leading under pressure, I'm uniquely qualified to guide leaders through this experience. I graduated from the United States Naval Academy in 1991. I was first assigned to the USS Monongahela as a Surface Warfare Officer, where I served as Assistant Operations Officer. In 1993, I began Basic Underwater Demolition/SEAL training. After graduating, I served as an Assistant Platoon Commander at SEAL Team Four and Platoon Commander at SEAL Team One. Unfortunately, my career was cut short prematurely after sustaining injuries on deployment, and I was medically discharged from the Navy in 1999. Needing to find something to do with myself, I joined the private sector, where I excelled in sales and management. After 9/11, and after obtaining a medical clearance from my injuries as a Navy SEAL, I began working for the FBI in New York City in 2003, where I investigated terrorist groups from Afghanistan, Pakistan, India, and the Former Soviet Republics. In this role, I worked with law enforcement and intelligence agencies all over the world, investigating and combating terrorists. In 2012, I transferred to the Newark, New Jersey Field Office, where I investigated public corruption and violent street gangs.

During my time with the FBI while in New York City, I was a member of the New York SWAT Team. Being on the SWAT Team in the FBI is a collateral duty. As such, SWAT Team members are required to effectively carry out their duties as criminal investigators first and foremost. Despite being a "part-time" duty, the New York FBI SWAT Team was as good a combat unit I've ever been attached to. Because of my experience as a Navy SEAL and FBI SWAT Operator, I was deployed to Afghanistan in 2010 while an FBI Special Agent and attached to the US Army's 75th Ranger Regiment, where I saw extensive combat operations. Because of my conduct during these extensive combat operations, I was awarded the FBI's second highest award for valor, the Shield of Bravery.

While my resume may look impressive, the real power in my background comes not from the experiences I just shared with you, but from the number of mistakes and unmitigated screw-ups I experienced along the way. Lest you consider this false modesty, let me briefly explain.

My graduation from the Naval Academy survived two academic review boards for poor academic performance and several conduct review boards for less than conformist behavior, any of which could have ended my tenure at the school. The situation was similar when it came to my career as Naval Officer serving as both a Surface Warfare Officer (ship driver) and Special Warfare Officer (Navy SEAL). In both placements, I was on the brink of being asked to leave the Navy for conduct unbecoming an officer. Drinking, fighting, fraternization, insubordination. You name it, I did it.

I was not singled out in any of these instances. I earned the trouble that found me. The irony is that I was saved each time because I was also considered by many to be an excellent officer and leader. The dichotomy was striking and summed up by one senior officer, who pulled me aside one day to tell me this: "I won't be surprised if one day you are found drunk and dead in a ditch, or if you turn out to be one of the greatest officers this Navy has ever seen." For every time I heard that I was an excellent leader from either the enlisted men and women that I had the pleasure to lead or the Officers I served under, there was always the other side of the coin that followed, with something akin to, "Despite the stupid shit you do."

I had planned on spending my entire career in the SEAL Teams. It was not to be, though. During a deployment, I suffered a career-ending injury. In the 1990s, there was not a lot of work to go around for SEALs. As it would happen, I was injured on a rehearsal for an actual operation—a ship takedown. But even this "noble" exit had a dark side.

Two months prior, I had entered into a fly-by-the-seat of my pants marriage to a young lady I met in South America. She was Colombian and had never been to the United States before we were married. After my injury, both of my arms were in casts and I suffered frequent post-concussion headaches, so I was home a lot. This gave us the opportunity to engage in a never-ending series of arguments. What a shock! I mean, after all, we had known each other for a full two months or so. (Yes, I'm being a little sarcastic.)

Reputation is everything in the SEAL community. And while my behavior was inconsistent and somewhat self-sabotaging, I felt as though my reputation was in pretty good standing … until then.

As immature and feuding couples do, we looked for areas of weaknesses in the other to exploit and hurt. She did not have to look far to find mine—my Navy SEAL reputation. All it took was for her to make some calls to my SEAL Team Command and level some false accusations against me to begin to chip away at my reputation. On what seemed like a weekly basis, I would have to stand in front of my Commanding Officer and explain, "No, I did not lock her out of the house. No, I have not refused to support her financially. No, I am not shirking my duties as a husband and human being." After a while it got hard for my Command to believe me because the calls kept coming. Eventually, I had to bring in my lawyer to show that I had voluntarily ceded all of my paychecks (less about $300 a month for myself so I could eat) and voluntarily moved out of the house (while still paying the bills) resorting to sleeping on friends' couches and in my car.

After I brought in my lawyer, it was finally clear to my Commanding Officer that I was not doing the awful things

I was being accused of by my wife. However, in typical SEAL Team fashion, his response was clear and unambiguous. "What the fuck Lieutenant Doebler. Get your personal life in order."

The poor behavior exhibited by both my ex-wife and me certainly did not lead to a healthy environment for recovery during my medical leave and after. In fact, it led me to abuse my pain killing medication and subsequently struggle to get off them. This was my dirty little secret that did not help my cause one bit toward the end of my Navy SEAL career.

I spent extra time at the hospital after my daily rehabilitation sessions doing administrative tasks for hospital staff instead of heading back to the SEAL Team Command because I was so humiliated at what was happening. Rightfully, this did not sit well with my SEAL Team Command.

Here began the self-inflicted dismantling of my reputation. I was the one who decided to stay away because I wasn't courageous enough to face the embarrassment of what was happening in my personal life and how it was spreading to my professional life. My injuries were severe enough to be given a medical discharge. I accepted the medical discharge without a fight, finalized the ugliest of divorces, and left the SEAL Teams with my tail between my legs, feeling disgraced.

I could have stayed in the military, but my operating days would have been over. As it turned out, it took several years for the headaches to go away and get my strength back into my injured limbs. Men with worse injuries have stayed in the SEAL Teams to continue to add value in any way they could, so I did not have to leave. But I did. And like most people who are humbled by circumstances, I began the long process of self-reflection that has led me here.

After I left the SEAL Teams I started to reflect on my successes and failures. Why had I found success and why did I allow failure, or at least needless setbacks, to plague me unnecessarily? As I moved forward in life, I started to become acutely aware of not only what I was doing, but why I was doing it.

So much of what I had been operating on was emotion and intuition. Sometimes my emotions led me down the correct path, other times the wrong one. It was the same situation with my intuition. Sometimes it would bring great success, but I was not able to replicate it on a consistent basis.

Time, reflection, and maturity obviously play an important part in eliminating self-inflicted wounds, and as the years went on, that's exactly what I began to do: eliminate self-inflicted wounds. Through my time in the private sector and then in the FBI, I began to operate with more consistency. My stumbles came further and further apart and with far less severity … but they still came.

After 13 years of service, I left the FBI out of a massive frustration with its leadership. Unlike the SEAL Teams, where the expectation of good leadership is the norm and bad leaders are the outliers, the FBI is the opposite. It was my experience that poor leadership was the norm and good leaders were the outliers in the FBI. Even though some of the best leaders I've ever met worked in the FBI, this wasn't enough for me to stay. I decided it was time to put my money where my mouth was and either shut up and endure the leadership I disagreed with or leave. So, I left. After so many years of learning the hard way what it meant to be a leader, I could no longer stand watching and being subjected to the largely incompetent leadership in the FBI. I wanted to make a difference in the lives of leaders who wanted to change.

As I began the process of putting together my leadership consulting business I finally had to sit down and evaluate my life and decide where things went right and where things went wrong. More importantly, I had to figure out why things went right and why things went wrong.

In short, I came to realize that life was made up of a series of concepts that repeated themselves regardless of the situation. And then I realized that the concepts I was recognizing formed a process for leadership and general positive behavior. Every potential landmine in life, and its solution, could be found in this process.

My experiences, and deep reflection and analysis of them, have led me to the development of a leadership process that will help define what we as leaders hold ourselves and our teams accountable for. That leadership process is what you're about to learn in this book. It is not a series of "must dos," but instead a process that is flexible enough to fit anyone's personal circumstance, lifestyle, profession, or personality.

Because the leadership process is so flexible, we can say that there is an Art required to ensure each element meets the needs of your team, your family, or you. It is not a one-size-fits-all process. It requires thought, reflection, and artistry.

What's more, as I became interested in how the brain

works and how to use it to produce real behavioral change, I came to realize the elements of the leadership process follow the pattern needed to literally rewire your brain. I believe the scientific parallels lend credibility to the leadership process, beyond the fact that I developed the process from first-hand experience and not some theoretical model. I don't claim to be a scientific expert, but I do cite the scientific parallels for each element of the leadership process, so get ready for a little science.

Welcome to the Process, Art, and Science of Leadership. I have a leadership process that mirrors the science of behavioral change and requires artistry to make it relevant. If you don't believe your circumstances are applicable to one of the elements of my leadership process, you can look to the science behind it for validation.

I truly believe if I had been exposed to the Process, Art, and Science of Leadership as a young man, I would have avoided a lot of unnecessary hardship—hardships I caused for myself and to those around me who loved and supported me. This process was built on the good, the bad, and the ugly experiences of my life, a life that's been flawed but also obsessed with what it means to be a good leader. I hope that you find what you need within these pages.

CHAPTER ONE

The Leadership Process Overview ... and Cold Exposure

LEADERSHIP IS NOT EASILY DEFINED. ASK TEN PEOPLE FOR the definition of leadership and you will likely get ten different answers. Likewise, ask ten people what leaders do, and you are likely to get ten different answers. And all of these answers, by the way, may be accurate to one degree or another.

Similarly, the language and concepts we use in leadership present the same ambiguity. But they shouldn't. The concepts of leadership are simple. A leader must have full situational awareness, which gives them the ability to make good decisions with a full understanding of the situation at hand. Additionally, a leader must make it clear what they will hold their people accountable to. While these concepts may be simple, the fact is that good, effective leadership takes a little more work than this.

Great leaders don't ignore the emotions and experiences of themselves or their teams. Great leaders don't assume their people will know what they are being held accountable for. Great leaders don't hope their people will know what they are supposed to do. Great leaders don't rely on assumption and hope.

Great leadership and continuity among teams requires something that is rarely found: a common leadership language based in process.

The process I'm about to introduce to you creates a common leadership language that allows leaders to define what they will hold their people accountable to. The key elements of the process will always remain constant. The beauty of this leadership process is that it allows for artistry and flexibility to account for a leader's individual personality, current and emerging needs, and static and dynamic environments. It is a process each leader can make their own while ensuring their team is speaking a common leadership language. It is a process that allows leaders to toe the correct side of the line that separates chaos and order; two states of being that are often separated by the thinnest of margins in the world of the leader.

This process consists of five elements, with each element effectively building off the one before it. The five elements are:

1. Practice Emotional Awareness and Recognition
2. Practice Cultural Awareness and Recognition
3. Create Guidelines for Behavior
4. Implement the Planning Process
5. Meet the Resistance[1]

These are not five random, separate, and distinct principles. They all build on each other to create a common leadership language. Like any effective process, we cannot skip steps. If there is a distinct leadership behavior or concept you want to work on, it will find a home inside this process. In any leadership challenge you face, the solution will be found inside one of the key elements of this tried and true, battle-tested, leadership process.

Process is Not a Four-Letter Word

Some leaders feel that process is a dirty word. However, a process allows us to identify where things went right and where things went wrong. When we can clearly identify where our endeavors and initiatives went right or wrong, we can identify specifically what we should continue doing and what aspects need adjustments. If we act on instinct or gut alone, without imposing any kind of structure or strategy, we'll never be able to quickly and accurately identify where negative behaviors or actions are limiting our ability to accomplish objectives.

People shy away from the word "process" because it feels too confining. They don't like to feel as if their options for action are limited. Even though we can all agree that behavioral guidelines (one of the elements of the process I'm sharing with you) are necessary for effective leadership, how do we decide which behaviors are appropriate for each individual workplace? Isn't it possible that certain behaviors are necessary for some but not for others? Should some behaviors always be in place or can they change? In the context of these questions, process can feel as if it's stifling instead of helpful.

That's where the Art of leadership comes in. Deciding what goes inside each of the elements of the leadership process will vary from person to person and group to group. There will be a certain fluidity and flexibility required to find your sweet spot, and then the sweet spot is likely to change.

You may believe that some behaviors, for example, should always be in place no matter what. Good! It's your canvas; paint how you see fit. It is not my intention to tell you which behaviors to implement. It is my intention to stress the importance of establishing behaviors and then offer suggestions, guidance, and anecdotes to help you in your decision process.

Steps 1 & 2: Practice Emotional and Cultural Awareness and Recognition

Our leadership process begins with awareness. If leadership is nothing at all, it is the ability to make good decisions based on a full knowledge of the situation at hand. Leaders must be aware of what they are doing and how they are acting. And since emotions drive our actions, we must master Emotional Awareness and Recognition; the first element of the leadership process.

In the first element, we focus on awareness and recognition of our emotions. In the second element of the leadership process, we focus on awareness and recognition of our cultures; what we and those around us do ... without judgement, for better or for worse.

By definition, culture is made up of the things we do, not the labels we put on them. It's fine to say you have a culture of, say, excellence. But too many teams, organizations, and leaders stop there, and that is unacceptable. If you can't define or articulate the things you do that create excellence, then you don't have a culture of excellence. All you have is a meaningless label.

Before we do anything, we must first identify what we do that makes up our culture. Not what we should do. Not what we want to do. What we actually do. And we must define it without judgement, for better or for worse.

A word of warning: The first two elements of the leadership process will be the hardest to master and the hardest to swallow. But they are the foundation of great leadership. Awareness of how we feel (which drives our actions), and awareness of what we do (that makes up our culture), will define how we behave as leaders. Without this awareness, we cannot make the necessary adjustments toward personal and professional improvements.

Step 3: Create Guidelines for Behavior

Now that we have done the work of being aware of our emotions, cultures and therefore actions, we can begin the process of defining what we will do, or how we will behave, by establishing the third element of the leadership process: Guidelines for Behavior.

This is where the rubber meets the road in the leadership process. This is where accountability and action live. Remember, you can't hold someone accountable if they don't know what they are supposed to be accountable for. Guidelines for

Behavior is where we begin to define what we will hold people accountable for.

The measure for creating Guidelines for Behavior lies in this basic premise:

If you didn't change the way you made, marketed, or sold your widget, but behaved in these ways, would you get better?

If the answer is "yes," then you have established good Guidelines for Behavior.

Step 4: Implementing the Planning Process

The situational awareness outlined in Elements One and Two of the process, along with establishing behavioral guidelines in Element Three, are crucial building blocks for leadership. But ultimately, leaders act to get results. Leaders don't act randomly. They act in a disciplined and methodical fashion. They properly delegate after defining objectives. They are able to question actions while still fostering initiative and autonomy in their people.

Leaders do this by having a plan. The fourth element of the leadership process covers the elements of a tried-and-true, battle-tested planning process. Cover the elements of the planning process and you will find mission success. And at the same time, you will create a team of thinkers who act with initiative, autonomy, and precision.

Step 5: Meeting The Resistance

My leadership process is simple and based in common sense. If you embrace and implement its elements you will find leadership success. Yet the people you lead, and even you at times, will resist it. Why? "The Resistance" is that unexplainable force of nature that stops us from doing the things we know we should be doing.

The elements of the leadership process will help you identify where The Resistance is coming from and how you can overcome it, both in the people you lead and in yourself. In the end, The Resistance will mostly come down to using a very basic behavior that will allow you to face it in a constructive, methodical fashion, void of overly emotional behaviors or feelings.

Finding Calm Amidst the Chaos

I mentioned calm and chaos toeing opposite sides of the same line in the beginning of this introduction. It's true. And the ability to fall on the correct side of this line as a leader lies in our ability to know the leadership process and then use the art to ensure we have made the process something that fits our unique needs and personalities, as individuals.

So much of leadership comes down to how you personally react under stress and pressure. Throughout this book, I'll be walking you through the five-step process above. But I'll also be challenging you through physical exercises so you can learn firsthand how you hold up under novel and uncomfortable situations. I'll be teaching you to use cold exposure and breathing techniques as tools to identify and practice the art of leadership. The method created by Wim Hof, the Dutch extreme athlete, uses cold exposure, breathing, and mindset to transform you physiologically, mentally, and emotionally. Lest you plan to write this off as some New Age hippie propaganda, all of the benefits of the Wim Hof Method are backed by extensive scientific evidence.

So, what does the Wim Hof Method have to do with leadership? For my part, I began learning the benefits of breathing and cold exposure from Wim Hof in 2017 and received my instructor certification in his method in 2018. In so many ways, breathing and cold exposure have changed my life and my health—those are a given. But in so many ways, I have also found that they have great leadership applications. The cold and the discomfort make the voices inside our heads loud, which creates a chaotic environment, both literally and figuratively. How do we calm ourselves while in an ice bath? How do we calm those voices in our head? How do we create order and calm amidst the chaos of the cold and our inner demons?

We will use breathing and cold exposure as an intellectual and physical tool to help us become better leaders and better human beings. The leadership process will help us manage the chaos/order continuum we battle as leaders. Breathing and cold exposure will help us practice elements of the leadership process so we can begin to change our mindset and the way we see, and react, to chaos and turn it into order and calm.

The five elements of the process: Practicing Emotional Awareness and Recognition, Practicing Cultural Awareness and Recognition, Creating Guidelines for Behavior, Implementing the Planning Process, and Meeting the Resistance, will establish your leadership language. That language will create a predictability around the environment. When people are part of a safe, predictable environment where behaviors and expectations of them are clear and unambiguous, individuals and teams thrive.

CHAPTER TWO

Element One— Emotional Awareness and Recognition

WELCOME TO THE MOST DIFFICULT ELEMENT OF THE leadership process. Emotional Awareness and Recognition will challenge you and in many cases, frustrate you, in every aspect of your life.

We as human beings daily give so little regard to our emotions. We've come to believe that we've got a handle on it or that we've got more important things to concern ourselves with than something as trivial and juvenile as our emotions. We may even consider paying attention to and acknowledging our emotions as a sign of weakness.

Here is the quick answer as to why Emotional Awareness and Recognition is essential to great leadership: Emotions drive our actions and our actions drive our results. As leaders we are judged by our actions; what we do, what we say, and the results we achieve.

If we want to be in control of the things we do and say that impact organizational success or failure, then we must be hyper aware of the very thing that drives our actions—our emotions. Without this, mission accomplishment may as well be left to a flip of the coin.

Emotions Influence Both Our Outer and Inner Worlds

Research tells us that we have between 60,000-70,000 thoughts in one day and 80 to 90% of those thoughts are the same as the day before.[2] For most people, 70% of the time those thoughts are associated with the hormones and emotions of stress: anger, jealousy, frustration, worthlessness, fear, anxiety, insecurity, guilt, envy, etc.[3] [4]

Every time you have a thought, your brain literally sends a chemical through the body to match how you feel with how you think.[5] [6] This creates a cycle between the mind and body better known as the mind/body connection. When you begin to feel the way you think, you begin to think the way you feel, the body creates more of those chemicals, and the cycle continues.[7] Unfortunately, the cycle continues with the same thoughts over and over, most of which are those associated with the emotions of stress.

In stress, you are in fight, flight, or hide mode. When we are in stress mode, activating our sympathetic nervous system, our body sends blood to our extremities because that is where we need the energy to fight, run, or hide. This is a good thing in the short term because it helps us stay alive. However, when stress is our sustained state of being the heart starts to function incoherently. Then the heart begins to send inconsistent messages to the brain, and we begin to move into a state of imbalance or dis-ease.[8] [9] [10]

Experiences create emotions. As human beings, we do not distinguish between an actual experience that creates an emotion or an emotion that can be created by thought alone.[11] [12] [13] To our body and brain it is the same thing. So again, if 80 to 90% of our thoughts are the same as the day before, your mind and body will believe they are in the same past experience all the time. It ultimately has nothing to do with the current event or experience. It's about the emotion that is created from the event or experience because the emotion will emanate and begin to define you from the past experience.

When you learn something new, the neurons in your brain make new synaptic connections.[14] It's a phenomenon in neuroscience called neuroplasticity, which tells us that physical and chemical changes take place in the brain from every new thought, choice, experience, and emotion.[15] [16] To remember the new information, we must continue to revisit it … like we revisit those emotions of stress day after day. When we do this those synaptic connections in the brain become stronger and stronger, for better or for worse.

We very rarely get past our analytical brain on a day-to-day basis.[17] We are constantly thinking about what happened earlier in the day or yesterday and what we need to do next. When we are doing this during our workday it creates a stress response that activates our sympathetic nervous system or our fight or flight responses. This is all ok; we need this to survive.[18] [19] But when this is all we do, all day every day, the science of epigenetics tells us that this constant stress downregulates our genes. When genes are downregulated we get sick. In short, our thoughts (what happened yesterday or this morning, what we need to do later, etc.) can make us sick.[20]

About 5% of people are born with true genetic disorders. About 95% of people who walk into a healthcare facility do so because of a stress-related disorder.[21] Now that we know when we experience an emotion the brain sends a chemical to the body, and that we think the same thoughts as the day before 90% of the time, we can rightly conclude that we become chemically-addicted to our emotions.[22] And we know that the majority of us are acting on the emotions of stress about 70% of the time.

In essence, we use the problems and conditions in our lives to reaffirm our addiction to our emotions. We find something in every interaction or experience that allows us to feel the way we've conditioned our mind and body to feel. We literally turn on the stress response by thought alone.[23] [24]

And because the stress response downregulates genes and this makes us sick, we rightly conclude that our thoughts and emotions can make us sick. Or, at least the wrong, sustained emotions, like those of stress. The evidence suggests the opposite is true as well. Elevated emotions like those of love, gratitude, abundance, and worthiness can upregulate our genes and make us well.[25]

The Importance of Self-Reflection

Every good leadership process starts with self-reflection. Recognizing your emotions will allow you to act in a way that is in your control, not in a way that is in the emotion's control.

Our goal here is not to understand why you have the emotions you have. I do believe it's worth it for everyone at some point to understand the cause of their underlying emotions, especially the negative ones that drive us to act outside of our best interest or outside of our best self. For some, this can be an exhaustive process that may take years to get your arms around. But again, this is not our goal right now. Recognizing your emotions and understanding where they come from are two different conversations. We are focusing on recognizing our emotions so we can control our actions and make good, sound leadership decisions when that emotion shows itself.

As a leader, you must focus on the effect your emotions have on your actions. When we recognize our emotions, we can begin the process of understanding, and controlling, what our actions will be going forward. We are leaders, so we must focus on the effect our emotions have on our actions. Regardless of whether we understand the deep-seated root and cause of our emotions, we will still have them so we have to be aware of them to ensure they do not control our decision-making process.

We are also not here to judge our emotions. You are allowed to have the emotions you have whether you like what they are or not. Be at home with that notion! Again, where your emotions come from, how you feel about them, and how you act on them are all separate conversations. However, unlike the challenge of finding the deep-seated root of your emotions, recognizing your emotions and the actions they drive may begin to have a therapeutic effect on how you feel about your least desirable emotions. Minimally, you will eventually be able to dance with your unwelcomed emotions when you realize you can control how you respond to them simply by being aware of them.

In short, the leader is aware of his or her emotions and then acts on them appropriately and consciously.

Where Do We Start?

Let's start by breaking down the word itself to give full clarity as to what we're discussing. The breakdown of the word "emotion" tells us all we need to know. The root of the word is from the Latin verb "to move." The prefix "e" connotes to "move away." Very simply, this breakdown suggests that a tendency to act is implicit in every emotion. Let's look at a few actions and some potential corresponding emotions.

How about when we procrastinate, or exercise in-action? This type of behavior can be fueled by many emotions. Perhaps we have an underlying fear of the task at hand. Perhaps we feel overwhelmed at what lies before us. Or, maybe we are simply indifferent or bored at the prospect of what we need to do.

Fear, overwhelmed, bored, indifferent. All are various forms of emotions that drive in-action or procrastination. If in an honest moment you asked yourself, "Why am I procrastinating?" your answer will lie somewhere inside an underlying emotion.

Let's look at cruelty or anger as an action. Why are people cruel? A lot of times people are cruel because they feel jealous of someone. People sometimes act angrily because they feel insecure or unsure of themselves, so they overcompensate with anger or even arrogance. Again, all the answers as to why you are acting a certain way will lie somewhere inside an underlying emotion.

The theory of emotions driving our actions is simple; it's common sense. If we want to be in control of our actions, we must first be aware of the emotions that drive them. So now the hard part. How do we develop the ability, or habit, of Emotional Awareness and Recognition?

If leadership is nothing else, it is situational awareness; the ability to make good decisions based on a full knowledge of the situation at hand. For all the reasons we just outlined regarding emotions, situational awareness must begin with ourselves. We cannot be situationally aware if we are not in the moment, fully present and aware of what we are feeling and doing during every interaction we have and every task we are undertaking.

For now, we are going to put the importance of being in the moment aside (we'll discuss it in a later chapter). Just keep the concept in the back of your mind until then. To be aware of what we are feeling, what our emotions are, we must always be in the here and now.

Like It Or Not, the Emotion Will Not Be Ignored

Unacknowledged emotions live in our unconscious mind, which is different from our subconscious mind.[26] When we consciously walk away from a problem we are struggling to solve, we let our subconscious mind get to work. It's those times when, BAM! the solution just came to you. That's your subconscious mind working for you.

Unfortunately, those unacknowledged emotions housed in our unconscious mind aren't getting the same treatment. It is easy to acknowledge and embrace good, positive emotions. We see children or puppies playing and we smile at the joy and innocence. There is no reason to deny or put aside that joyful emotion.

But, what about the more troubling or negative emotions that enter our world? What do we do with those? Envy, anger, jealousy, anxiety, fear, worthlessness, guilt. What happens when we allow ego to take over and we deny we are feeling what we are feeling, as we typically do with those types of negative emotions? Or, when we ignore those emotions and bury them because that is the "strong" thing to do? What about when we push them to the side because it is beneath us to acknowledge those pesky emotions? Only weaklings acknowledge emotions, right?

Our body and our mind are the most amazing machines ever made. Everything that is a part of us has a purpose. So, when we feel an emotion, it serves a purpose. If we choose not to acknowledge something we've created, like an emotion, we don't get to just pull it out of our ear and put it on a shelf.

The body is a closed system. That emotion you are denying is going to be housed somewhere and that somewhere is in your unconscious mind, and it is not going to just lie dormant until you decide you want to deal with it. The emotion will manifest itself in some way. It will be either some physical or emotional manifestation that you'll act on. And, if we act on an emotion that is sitting in our unconscious mind, it is an action without a conscious understanding of what it is we are acting on.

When this happens, we are employing hope as a strategy. All you can do is hope your action will be appropriate because you are unaware of the underlying emotion driving the action. When you are unaware of the underlying emotion driving your action, you are powerless to make a conscious decision about how you want to act on your emotion.

This is the process most people use when it comes to acting on their emotions: TRIGGER to EMOTION to ACTION.[27] Something happens that triggers an emotion and they then immediately act on that emotion.

Here is the process leaders use: TRIGGER to EMOTION to THINK and DECIDE to ACT.[28] Something happens that triggers an emotion and leaders recognize the emotion driving them to act, think about how they want to act, make a decision, and then act. But you can't add THINK and DECIDE if you are not aware of the inherent driver of your action—your emotion.

The (Potentially) Deadly Consequences of Unacknowledged Emotions

When I went to free-fall jump school as a Navy SEAL we went through extensive instruction before we actually jumped out of an airplane. None of it was overly complicated, but it was all important for obvious reasons.

We learned our body positions so we could fall through the air in an appropriate and controlled manner. And, among other things, we learned the protocols before we pulled our parachute, which were pretty simple: Check your altimeter, look left, look right, look up, and look down to ensure you have clear air space, and pull your ripcord. Again, not exactly rocket science.

I walked to the airplane for my first jump full of bravado and borderline arrogance. In my mind I was super calm, super confident ... Superman! The next thing I remember was falling through the air aimlessly and watching the instructor reach for my ripcord to pull it for me. I ended up getting to my ripcord first, but I had essentially blown through all my protocols and eventually pulled my parachute at the minimum safe altitude, or probably even a little below. In short, a disastrous and unsafe first jump that put those around me at risk.

My instructor was very clear when we met on the ground, "If you have one more performance like that, I'll make sure you never jump out of an airplane again." A tough proposition given that the SEAL in Navy SEAL stands for Sea, Air, and Land Soldier. It would be difficult for me to fulfill the "Air" portion of my job description if I was not able to jump from an airplane. He concluded his remarks by telling me I had twenty minutes to re-pack my parachute and be on the plane for the next jump. Essentially, twenty minutes to save my career.

That next 20 minutes needed complete clarity and honesty

if I was to fix the situation. It was an honesty and clarity that made clear to me that the bravado and arrogance I was exhibiting prior to the jump was false, it was a lie. I was not super confident. I was not super calm. I certainly was not Superman. I was one thing and one thing only, afraid. My action based on my underlying, unacknowledged emotion of fear was inaction. Inaction is not exactly a great draw for an "action" when you are jumping out of an airplane.

That's my point. Unacknowledged emotions create actions that we are not aware of until after the fact, if at all. Becoming aware after the fact, like what happens to many of us, can be too late to avoid a damaging result, like when you are jumping out of an airplane. My process in this example was TRIGGER (jumping out of an airplane) to EMOTION (fear) to ACTION (inaction).

But a funny thing happened when I acknowledged my fear. It brought the emotion from my unconscious mind, the place where unacknowledged emotions go to wreak havoc on us, to my conscious mind. Now it was in a place where I could include "THINK and DECIDE" to my process and therefore make a conscious decision about what action I wanted to take. Simply acknowledging the emotion allowed me, not the emotion, to be in control of my action. And that is exactly what I did, take control of the action.

I completed my next jump, the entirety of the course, and the rest of my jumps in the SEAL Teams in excellent fashion. It does not matter that I never lost the fear of jumping. In fact, I made sure to acknowledge and embrace the fear before every jump because doing so ensured I was focused on the details to keep myself and, more importantly, those around me, safe.

I did not concern myself with the fact that after so many jumps I still rehearsed all my protocols right up until the moment we jumped from the aircraft. At some point, in any endeavor, familiarity can breed a certain laissez faire attitude. Among other seasoned operators, continuing to physically rehearse all my protocols on the plane before the jump tended to look a little out of place.

I could have been at risk of falling back into my original trap of overcompensating for my fear by acting with that same bravado and arrogance from my very first jump. I knew, however, that I could not trust that instinct. I had to focus on being aware of the emotion, thinking and deciding how I wanted to act, and then focusing on the actions I decided on. In other words, I decide on my actions, not the emotion.

Combat provides a heightened awareness of the consequences of our actions, but also shows that the decision-making process for every decision we make is the same, or at least should be the same; TRIGGER to EMOTION to THINK and DECIDE to ACT.

Many different things can happen inside of THINK and DECIDE. We can think about the Behavioral Guidelines we've established for ourselves or the Planning Process; elements of the leadership process we will cover in detail later. The bottom line, though, is that I was able to focus on the protocols I was taught despite the fear I felt. And the simple reason is because I moved the emotion that was not allowing me to do this from my unconscious mind to my conscious mind where I could evaluate the situation and make a conscious decision about how to proceed.

It's About the Conscious Decision, Not the Right Decision

As you can see, not acknowledging your emotions can be a recipe for disaster. Whether it be a matter of life or death like it could have been in my combat jumping example, or a series of small, seemingly insignificant poor or unconscious actions that build up over time.

This does not guarantee we'll always make the right choice. The aim is to make sure you are making a conscious choice. If you make a bad decision, at least now you have a decision-making process to look back on and examine where you went wrong. This process will allow you to make positive adjustments for the next time.

Even when we make the wrong choice, based on a conscious decision, we win. We win because you made a decision to go with your instinct and then you were able to evaluate whether your instinct was good or bad.

As leaders we can't hope or assume we will make the right choice on how to act. As leaders, we put ourselves in a position to take conscious action by always being aware of the driving force behind our actions; our emotions.

CHAPTER THREE

One Side of the Emotional Coin ... Actions into Negative Consequences

Our Reactions to Our Emotions Are Just as Important

We all have our own unique demons when it comes to emotions. Sometimes those demons come from how we feel about our emotions. Yes, we have emotions about our emotions and very often those are the ones eating away at us in our unconscious mind.

For instance, perhaps you have a particularly challenging relationship with a family member, like a parent. Perhaps they make you angry. You might even have acknowledged, publicly or privately, that they make you angry. Yet, you can't seem to break the chains of your anger, or at least how you act on your anger.

You go through the process: TRIGGER (my mother makes me so mad when she talks to me like that!) to EMOTION (anger) to THINK and DECIDE (I want to act courteously and with a smile on my face towards her) to ACT (you act accordingly and your Sunday dinner is without incident, but you are not feeling any better about the situation and the tension in the air is palpable).

You go through the process and the tension seems to build with every day and every interaction. You find yourself short and tense with your own family, friends, or co-workers. You seem to find the same anger or frustration you have with your mother everywhere. The process isn't working!

You're right, the process may not work in this case because anger isn't the emotion seated in your unconscious mind. You are not leaving anger unacknowledged in this scenario, so your anger probably isn't the problem. Who doesn't get angry or short with their parents from time to time for goodness sakes? What's more likely is the emotion you feel about your anger is wreaking havoc with you.

We generally expect to honor and respect our parents as we move through life. We also generally expect that we can put hard feelings of the past behind us, especially if we faced some adversity not of our own doing growing up. So, when we have these expectations of ourselves as mature and forgiving adults and we still feel angry towards Mom, we may really be feeling guilty about the anger we harbor. Or, we may be resentful of how we are continually treated and then in turn feel guilty about being resentful.

The same scenario can play out in many ways when it comes to how you feel about how you feel. Maybe you didn't get that promotion or recognition for a job well done and you feel frustrated about that. Or, perhaps you came up short on a big goal you set for yourself and you feel frustrated or deflated. It may not be the frustration in these cases you need to concern yourself with because you are likely very in tune to that emotion. However, it may be a sense of worthiness you are struggling with. Perhaps you don't feel worthy of success and you are further embarrassed, ashamed, and insecure about that very feeling of unworthiness.

My point is simple. Look beyond the initial emotion to get to your unconscious mind because those emotions—how we feel about how we feel—can cut deep and wreak havoc on us.

Your question is likely, "Ok, what now? Yes, I feel guilty about being angry, now what?" Patience. One step at a time. Remember, each element builds on the one before it. For now, be aware of and recognize the emotion. It's the first and most important step. It cannot be skipped.

A Cautionary Tale

Without directly "addressing" emotions, my tenure in the SEAL Teams was full of emotional awareness and recognition. Regular respect was paid to emotions for battlefield evaluations, how you handled a short timeline, or stressful personal interactions of any kind. In short, if you acted on an emotion of stress you could count on quickly being called out to get your shit together, plain and simple. The expectation of calm, methodical, and unemotional thought and action was the expectation of every SEAL, not just the leadership.

I also worked as an FBI Special Agent primarily out of its "Flagship Office," New York City. The FBI is the self-proclaimed "World's Premier Law Enforcement Organization." While some of the best leaders I've ever worked with, worked for, or observed were FBI Special Agents, my caveat to that is that they were the outliers. The expectation of great leadership was the norm in the SEAL Teams. In the FBI, the expectation was the opposite. Poor emotionally charged leadership was the expectation and norm in the FBI.

When I investigated violent street gangs, I began an investigation into a group that had run rampant over a community for at least a decade. Various low-level arrests had taken place over the years, but none of them put a dent into the capacity of the gang to own the streets. This is primarily because the leadership of the gang did a good job of buffering itself against the efforts of law enforcement, leaving the lower level operators to suffer the consequences of law enforcement actions.

My partner and I had recruited a well-placed source who had close relationships to many of the gang's most established and tenured members. Because of the source's access, we were able to infiltrate the gang with more than one undercover FBI employee. We did this through the source's introduction of the Undercovers to some mid-level, well-established gang operatives. To my knowledge from reading about the various investigations into this gang over at least a ten-year period, to include State, Local, and Federal investigations, there had never been one Undercover introduced into the gang. I cannot even recall reading about one well-placed source in the investigations. In a relatively short period of time, we were well entrenched into the gang with well-placed sources and Undercovers.

Our goal was to get access to the gang's leadership so we could effectively cut the head off the snake. Once we had successfully infiltrated the gang, one of the Undercovers recommended a different tact to getting to the leadership of the gang. It was a tact he had successfully used before and seen work on another occasion.

Instead of going the traditional route of starting with small, low-level drug buys in the hopes of moving up the ranks and eventually reaching the highest levels of the gang leadership, the Undercover recommended that we buy large quantities of drugs immediately. The Undercover believed that the strength of the introduction into the gang from the source, as well as several successful interactions with various members of the gang by the Undercovers, put us in a unique position to try this risky approach. We had successfully completed a couple of obligatory "test buys." This is where everyone is at their most cautious to ensure law enforcement is not playing a hand in the game. All was good. Now it was time to up the ante.

The Undercover's logic was sound: If we distinguished ourselves from low-level operatives, we would likely get the attention of the gang leadership quickly. They would hear about the large orders and begin to do their due diligence about the new players in town. They would most certainly inquire who introduced the Undercovers into the gang, how long the Undercovers had been around, where they were from, and the status of the buys already made. We were more than covered on all these fronts. One way or the other, we would know if we were going to get access to the leadership in a relatively short period of time. I agreed with the Undercover's idea wholeheartedly and prepared to present the plan to my boss.

This strategy was the epitome of risk/reward. From a purely administrative perspective, when you start with small, low-level drug buys and don't get anywhere, very little money is likely lost, and it is chalked up to the price of doing business. However, if you come out of the gate with large purchases that require large amounts of money, and you don't gain any traction ... well, understandably people in high places in the FBI will notice and ask questions.

What's more, while drugs were a sadly obvious way to begin buying from the gang, we wanted guns to be our focus. Gun violence was rampant, and we were now connected with the very players who were using and supplying the guns and, literally and figuratively, killing the community. We wanted to employ the same strategy with guns as we did with drugs; buy big early. This was all in a bid to force the gang leadership to pay attention with the hopes of meeting them directly and begin making a long-term dent in the gang's activity, or stopping it outright. Risk/reward operations should come with lofty expectations and we had them. Or, at least, some of us did.

Enter "Tim"

My plan was met with resolute dismissal by my immediate supervisor, whom I will call Tim. After I finished briefing Tim on our concept of operations, he went on to condescendingly describe the bottom-up strategy of gang work. We pursue low-level drug buys in the hopes of rising up the chain of command and maybe even getting up on a wire. I acknowledged Tim's strategy because there is a general playbook to these types of investigations that should always be looked at first.

However, I went on to explain to Tim how that strategy had been ineffective against this gang at curbing the violence and treachery it had inflicted on the community for many years. Furthermore, I informed Tim that these investigations had been conducted by Local, State, and Federal Law Enforcement agencies to include the FBI. Again, I added, investigations by all levels of law enforcement that ended with very little success. Even more, guns had not been addressed in prior investigations. It was time to change things up, I argued.

Tim's response? "It's reckless and you're going to get the Undercovers killed."

I then went on to explain that the idea was generated by one of the Undercovers and that he felt completely safe given the validity of his introduction into the gang and the relationship he had built with the gang members up to that point. Further, the Undercover had previously, and successfully, conducted a separate operation with the same general concept of operations and felt we were in a better position to execute our plan than his previous operation. I even recommended Tim speak directly with the Undercover. Perhaps the Undercover could explain the plan better than I was explaining.

Tim ignored the logic in my argument and refused to speak directly to the Undercover. Still ever-so-condescendingly, Tim told me that the entire plan was a waste of time because it would never get approval above his level. Even in a parallel universe where my plan did get approved, Tim was absolutely certain Headquarters would never approve that amount of money for ONE purchase of drugs and weapons. "Ludicrous," Tim declared!

I might have further inflamed the situation by advising Tim the plan called for several large purchases of drugs and weapons, not just one. Words cannot describe the look on Tim's face when I hit him with that one.

I further explained that I had already run the idea by the person at Headquarters who would ultimately make the decision of money approval and was advised I would very likely get the money approved based on what I had told him. Tim was not happy with my "insubordination" for running the idea by the "money approver" without his knowledge. I told Tim that it only made sense for me to talk with the approvers before we wasted time putting in the formal request and based on my conversation the money would likely get approved! So, Tim stuck to the notion that the operation itself would never get approved. My response was simple, "Let me request it and let's find out. If it doesn't get approved, I'll let it go."

Given Tim's opposition to my plan, I asked that he let me brief the operation and field all questions. Tim agreed to let me brief. But he also went about the business before the brief of making his opposition to the operation known to his boss, who would ultimately have the final approval decision. Tim was also not shy about letting everyone in the office know how dangerous my plan was, how reckless I was, and how briefing the plan was a waste of time because it would never get approved.

Well, the operation was approved. Needless to say, Tim was not happy and began explaining to anyone who would listen, including the investigators who were assisting me in the operation, that I was going to get someone killed. Not exactly confidence-inspiring behavior on the leader's part, to say the least.

What Has Happened So Far

Let's break here and reflect on some actions based on Tim's emotions. Tim showed himself almost immediately by flatly rejecting my proposal of big money buys early. Based on the things Tim said to me, it was clear he had never taken this investigative tact before, nor had he seen it done before. If he had, I'm quite certain he would have mentioned it. And if he had, he would have been able to explain the problems in my plan. Instead, he went immediately to name calling (reckless) and his anticipated outcome (I would get the Undercover killed). He then took the additional step of bad-mouthing me and my plan to those who were going to be directly involved in the operation. I know he did this because they told me (as if it weren't painfully obvious anyway ...) and I walked in on him in the act on at least one occasion.

Being resistant to my plan wasn't the problem. How Tim showed his resistance was the problem.

Which emotions drove Tim's actions? I can only speculate, but I'm sure this behavior sounds familiar to some of you. Nobody who is secure in their position as a leader, or human being, goes right to insult and innuendo as their default mode of action. So, my speculation is that Tim's insecurity, as a leader and person, was at the root of his actions.

To be sure, there were risks involved in this operation. The Undercover would be meeting with murderers on a regular basis, would be carrying large sums of cash, and buying weapons and drugs. His only backup—me and the other members of the operation—would be blocks away and not likely in a position to save his life should one of the gang members quickly decide it was time for the Undercover to be robbed and killed.

If the risks cannot be mitigated, then opposition to the plan and overall operation is warranted. This was not the case. Suffice it to say, I was able to articulate how the risk would be mitigated. Agree with my premise on risk mitigation or not, I always fully acknowledged that there was a chance the Undercover could be robbed, injured, or killed. Most importantly, the Undercover acknowledged there was a chance he could be robbed, injured, or killed. But we both understood, and agreed, that bearing risk was part of the job description and that we had accounted for every reasonable scenario that could put the Undercover at that risk. Tim struggled here. Tim was averse to any real risk, regardless of the planning and circumstances in place to mitigate it.

What is another term for risk aversion? Fear. If the emotion that drove Tim's actions was not insecurity, then it was fear. Fear of being associated with an operation that held true risk, perhaps.

Remember, the problem is not the inherent emotion(s) that Tim was feeling. It was the fact that he was reacting to and acting directly on the emotion. Gossiping, bad-mouthing, and innuendo are not the actions of someone who is conscious of recognizing an emotion and thinking before they act on it. These are especially not the actions of a leader.

What's more, Tim took the additional steps of continuing to bad-mouth the operation and, more specifically, me. Tim also did this at perhaps the worst possible times; during actual gun and drug buys.

"He's going to get ripped! He's going to get killed!"

The Undercover was wired for live transmission back to the office, which acted as a command post for the operation. The command post was manned by some FBI analysts and Tim.

In this instance, the Undercover had a large quantity of money on him and was scheduled to meet one of the most violent and longest-tenured members of the gang for our first large weapons purchase. The planning and preparation were thorough and contingencies, especially those related to the Undercover's safety, were accounted for. However, everyone knew of the inherent risks the operation held. The gang member could pull a weapon on the Undercover and rob him (aka, "rip" him), or worse, attempt to injure or kill him.

All members of the team in the field supporting the operation were well-aware of the risks but were conducting themselves like complete professionals. I oversaw the overall movement of team members and communications in the field, which was being transmitted real time back to the command post.

Despite the professionalism being displayed by the team in the field, Tim was not able to control himself back at the command post. Tim was walking around the entire office, not just the part of the office designated as the command post, ranting, "He's (the Undercover) going to get ripped! He's going to get killed!"

Despite many meetings with dangerous gang members, all involving large sums of money, the Undercover was never "ripped" and his safety never came under question during a gun or drug purchase. However, Tim's behavior never really changed from that first buy. Tim continued to act in this manner during the entirety of the operation.

When mistakes were made (and there were mistakes by me, to be sure), Tim used these opportunities to either attempt to shut down the case or highlight my "disregard" for some form of safety or procedure. When mistakes are amplified to an unreasonable scope, morale and trust begin to break down, which is exactly what happened. In the end, despite a massive amount of weapons and drugs being purchased (all of which were audio and video recorded), a murder-for-hire offer being made, and a request of the gang's leader to finally meet with the Undercover in person, the case was shut down with only a single arrest to show for it, leaving those responsible for the devastation of a community in place.

Why did Tim act in such a way to ensure such discord was sewn throughout the entire operation? Why did Tim put the operators assisting me in the case in the position to take sides ... agreeing with him or me?

I have speculated that Tim was acting on emotions alone, without thinking about the actions his emotions were driving. I have speculated that perhaps Tim was experiencing some insecurity or fear that led him to act in such a divisive and irresponsible manner. With each success the operation saw, Tim seemed to grow more and more frustrated and in turn would seem to find additional things to unprofessionally criticize.

The Final Analysis

Tim was not wrong to feel the way he did. None of us are wrong to feel how we feel. The purpose of Emotional Awareness and Recognition is just that—recognition. We should never feel like we are not allowed to feel a certain way.

The purpose of emotional recognition is not to judge how we feel, but to ensure our emotion does not lead us to act in a way that is not in our control. Maybe I'm being too hard on Tim. Maybe he was completely conscious of his emotions and how he was acting on them. If that was the case, though, then we are experiencing some other serious leadership gaps on Tim's part.

In the end, Tim's actions reflected his emotions, which were driving his actions. His actions were not those of a leader; they were the actions of someone who simply feels and then acts with no regard for "THINK" and "DECIDE."

And because Tim did not have emotional recognition, his actions led to discord and divisiveness, not success. Tim did not hold himself accountable to his emotions or actions. He just acted ... and we failed.

Tim could have spoken to the Undercover to get a different perspective on the plan when it became clear he and I were not seeing eye to eye. Tim could have simply said he was not willing to be part of something that involved the type of risk the operation had. The list of things Tim could have done as a leader goes on and on. But as a leader, he chose to forgo "THINK and DECIDE," and used the "TRIGGER to EMOTION straight to ACTION" formula.

For my part, as the case went on and saw success after success, I could have done better to take my own advice. I knew Tim would continue to act overly emotional with each successive operation because that is what he did the entire time. Despite his opposition, I was getting my way. Operations were getting approved, money was getting approved, and we were collecting an incredible amount of evidence. However, I grew tired of arguing with him over every little detail. I grew tired of him bad-mouthing me constantly. And I grew tired of the wedge he was driving between the operators just by virtue of his role as supervisor.

So, instead of acknowledging my frustration and maintaining my professionalism, I began to taunt Tim during the latter part of the operation. Every time I proposed a new operation, he told me how terrible and dangerous it was, which seemed to be a weekly occurrence. I could have simply ignored the insults and continued briefing the plans and seeing success. Instead, though, I began to take the tact of asking Tim to disagree with everything I said and proposed operationally, because he was always wrong, and I was looking at his opposition as my good luck charm. I unnecessarily poured fuel on the fire and turned a harmless campfire into an inferno.

As such, this incident goes down as one of the most destructive instances of a leader not having Emotional Awareness and Recognition I have ever experienced. What was more disturbing was the number of allies Tim was able to recruit in his childish escapade, which goes to the fact that, for better or worse, the leader will set the behavioral tone. This story marked the end of my FBI career. The organization looked too familiar to me from a negative leadership and cultural perspective.

CHAPTER FOUR

Practicing the Other Side of the Emotional Coin ... With an Ice Bath

NO BEHAVIOR OPERATES IN A BUBBLE. IN OTHER WORDS, there are always residual effects to any behavior you exhibit, both good and bad. In this case, when you become adept at being emotionally aware and using that awareness to make conscious decisions as opposed to letting your emotions dictate your actions, you will begin to see that awareness in others.

Back a million years ago when I was a Navy SEAL Platoon Commander, my platoon failed its final exercise to determine our fitness for deployment. We failed because, during the operational briefing, I had left out the radio frequency we would be using to communicate with each other. The monitors let us complete the entire 2-day operation, only to tell us upon returning from the field that we had already failed the exercise after the briefing.

I was distraught, as well I should have been. It was inexcusable, and I was humiliated. The Commanding Officer came to my room after we had been notified of my failure. I don't know what he planned to say to me, but I don't think it was what he ended up saying to me.

He took one look at me and very calmly asked, "What happened?"

My response was simple, because there was really only one response to give in my mind. "I Fucked up. It's my fault. That's it. I have no excuse."

If he came to reprimand me, which I think he intended to do, he changed gears after taking stock of my emotional state. He saw that the last thing I needed was to be yelled at. There was clearly nothing he could do to me that I wasn't doing to myself, except fire me. And fire me was what I was sure was going to happen because I believed I deserved it. Instead he said, "Go do it again."

"The brief?" I asked.

"No, whole thing. You'll be given a new scenario in an hour. Good luck." He left.

Our platoon had not slept in two days, but our energy went through the roof and we began the planning, briefing, and execution process all over again.

A few days after we returned to home base the Commanding Officer called me into his office, along with his second in command, the Executive Officer. They shared with me how they couldn't recall ever having seen a briefing and operation go so well, from beginning to end. Well done!

And then, again, the Commanding Officer took stock of my emotions. It was clear to him that I was prepared to now absorb the ass-chewing I deserved for my initial failure. He saw this opportunity and let me have it.

The Commanding Officer saved my career and changed my life. Not because he gave me a second chance, but because he made the right leadership decision based on understanding my emotional state. He was entirely focused on me, in the moment, and weighed my failure against my reaction to my failure. He made a decision based on all the information he had available to him, not just on the one piece of information that I had failed.

At the same time, he raised my ability to operate on a higher level and brought me to my knees in a heap of humility and self-reflection. That's impact. That's massive impact! That's the type of leadership that disrupts the status quo. He understood the importance of recognizing emotions in others.

Would he have been justified in firing me? Yes, without question. But that is not the point being made here. Because of his ability to be in the moment and recognize emotions in others, he could certainly explain—with greater depth than a linear "pass/fail" criteria—why he had come to the decision he came to, whether you agreed with his ultimate decision or not.

He didn't move straight to consequence. He held me responsible by allowing me to account for my actions. He asked me a question, "What happened?" Based on my answer to his question, he decided on consequence; "Do it all again, now." For me, the consequence was a blessing, a second chance and a life lesson that endures to this day.

Practicing the Art Through Cold Exposure

Taking the time to practice anything can be difficult; even for the things we really care about. If you are reading this book you care about leadership and want to get better. But the topic begs a very simple question, "How do you practice leadership?"

If you want to get better at piano and maybe even one day try your hand at a recital, you spend time alone on the piano and practice. You make mistakes, work on them, make more mistakes, work some more, and ultimately get better. Through this work and practice you become ready for your recital. You don't just jump into the recital and make your mistakes there, you practice first!

Sure, when it comes to leadership we must try things real time and make mistakes along the way. It comes with the territory. But surely there must be a way to practice before we give something a try for real. Welcome to the use of cold exposure to practice your art of leadership!

As we begin to work with Emotional Awareness and Recognition, you can be sure of one thing: Before, during, and after you step into an ice bath ... you will have an emotion. And, you will probably have an emotion about that emotion.

When we get into the cold, we experience vasoconstriction; an environmental experience that will cause some discomfort in our extremities as our body does its work to push blood to our vital organs so we can stay alive. Our fingers and toes are not as important as our heart for life, so the body naturally restricts the blood flow to those areas when we enter the cold. Additionally, the cold hits our body as a sensation.

Vasoconstriction (a little pain in our extremities) and a cold sensation in our bodies; these are the things that happen when we step into the cold. However, the emotions you feel when you take an ice bath are not automatically attached with vasoconstriction and the sensation of cold. Vasoconstriction and the cold sensation are just things that happen. You are assigning the emotion to it, whatever the emotion is.

Right about now is when people begin to declare that they don't do well with the cold and hate it more than anyone else on earth. This declaration is an ACTION to your EMOTION that is being TRIGGERED by the thought of an ice bath or cold shower. For now, we'll put the excuses we make to not expose ourselves to the cold on hold until we hit the second element of the leadership process: Cultural Awareness and Recognition. Let's stay focused on the emotions.

Nobody enthusiastically just jumps into a cold shower. Trust me, I've taken ice baths consistently for years now and there is always trepidation or reticence. The initial emotions you have will not be deep-seated, they'll be logical. But you may not like them. Fear or anxiety will likely be the initial emotion, but you may want to explain it away because we don't like to acknowledge fear or anxiety because they are a challenge to our ego. And because of this, the secondary emotion may be a sense of shame. Shame that you are afraid or anxious, shame that you are afraid to admit it, and shame that you didn't face the fear or anxiety and get into the cold shower.

Fear or anxiety are obvious, but try to go one step further about how you feel about these emotions. These are likely the emotions that will cause you problems.

Afraid of what? Who knows and who cares? No matter what the inherent fear is, it can't be properly addressed until we move it from our unconscious mind to our conscious mind. The unaddressed emotion sitting in our unconscious mind wreaks havoc on our actions. We do and say things without thinking because the emotion is in control, not us.

When we acknowledge we are afraid, for example, we get to continue the conversation.

"Afraid of what?" you decide to ask yourself.

"Afraid of how I will react to the cold," you may answer.

"Well, how do you want to react to the cold?" you continue with yourself.

"With calmness, like it doesn't bother me. I don't want to look silly." Now we are getting somewhere!

"Well, how do you do that?"

"Errol said I will have a natural physiological response when I get into the ice bath, like when you lose your breath during a panic attack. But it happens to everyone, so I don't have to worry about that," you explain.

"OK, what else?" you press yourself.

"Then he told me to find my breath. Exhale. Focus on the breath and the breath only. In through the nose, gently exhale. Once I get control of my breath, I should find some comfort in the ice," you explain to yourself.

The conversation can go on and on … and it will, especially when it comes to stepping into an ice bath. The point is, though, that it is the awareness of the emotion that is allowing you to have this conversation with yourself. You may still choose to succumb to your fear, but at least it will be a conscious decision and not some ridiculous excuse like your reaction to the cold is worse than everyone else's.

You can live with a conscious decision, based on an honest recognition of an emotion, not to do something. At the very least, it gives you something to work on, a place to find growth.

How amazing is that?

Otherwise, you are simply the person who makes excuses for yourself and pretends everyone can't see through them. In your heart and in your unconscious mind, though, you know the truth. And this truth creates more unacknowledged emotions that lead to other behaviors you are not proud of or in control of. It is where we begin the all-too-common practice of beating ourselves up.

Find growth or more self-loathing? I'll choose growth by simply acknowledging my emotions.

Recognizing emotions and their potential effect on your behavior is a vital component to great leadership. Recognizing your emotions before you step into an ice bath is an amazing intellectual drill that will help you make identifying your emotions a habit.

I have stepped into countless ice baths, cold showers, and natural bodies of water in the dead of winter. Each time I do, I experience an emotion. The emotion before I do is typically,

"Ugh! Again?" Even after all this time, that is generally my initial emotion before I get in.

Sometimes it's excitement like, "Yeah! Get some!" Or a calm, focused state. But, generally ... "Ugh!"

But that initial emotion almost doesn't matter to me anymore. What's happened now is that I've begun to assign different emotions to the cold and I try to enter the cold independent of my initial reaction. I've assigned the sensation of cold as a catalyst to enter a deep, focused, meditative state. I recognize vasoconstriction as a temporary state of discomfort that is a sign that my veins and arteries are becoming stronger, which will allow my blood to flow more freely and easily throughout my body.

When I'm super-stressed, I imagine the sensation of cold literally zapping my stress away. When I'm super-relaxed, I imagine the sensation of cold taking my ability to focus in a chaotic state to a higher level. When I'm distracted, I imagine the sensation of cold sharpening my ability to refocus at a moment's notice.

I could go on and on about the emotions I feel before I enter an ice bath and once I'm in the ice bath. In short, I go through a series of emotions every time I get into an ice bath. These are my emotions. They are not right, they are not wrong. They are not necessarily what you should feel, but you can look to find these feelings if you like.

The point is, I can describe them vividly because I understand the need to recognize them so I act in a way that I'm happy with; that I'm conscious of. The reason I can do this is because I practice this drill regularly, every time I get into an ice bath. Now it is a habit that I employ every day and in every aspect of my life.

Simply put, practice recognizing your emotions by stepping into an ice bath or cold shower regularly. How regularly? The physiological effects of an ice bath can last up to five days.[29] But we are not talking about the physiological effects, we are talking about the emotional and psychological effects. So, let's not kid ourselves. If you want to create a habit, start doing it every day.

Where to start? Don't worry, if you've never touched cold water before you don't have to make your first experience a 32-degree ice bath. You can start by turning your shower to cold for 15 seconds right before you get out. You can start by putting your hand in a bowl of ice water for 30 seconds.

Remember, the drill here is to identify your emotions so you can act in a way you are comfortable with. If you are "gutting or gritting" your way through the cold you are missing the point. Guts and grit are good, but not how we want to go through our life all day every day. We want to find flow and calm.

Whether it's a cold shower, your hand in a bowl of ice water, or a full-fledged ice bath, there are some things that will naturally happen. You will experience that shocking, loss of breath, extreme inhale. Think of it as an induced panic attack. Or, should I say, recognize it as an induced panic attack (an emotion). Without recognizing your "panic attack" as an emotion, you may be inclined to simply jump out of the water. Or, in real life, let the "panic attack" control you.

When we take the time to understand our emotions, we can make a conscious decision to exit the cold. But a funny thing happens when we come to our emotional recognition; we decide we don't like the idea of succumbing to our fear once we have faced it, and we stay in the cold.

We decide we are in control of our actions, not the emotion.

We find our breath. We slow down our breathing. We replace the panic-inducing, staccato breathing pattern with long, slow nasal inhales. We exaggerate, initially, with long, slow exhales either through the mouth or the nose. Then we fall into a normal nasal breathing pattern and enjoy our heightened meditative state.

Now, imagine taking that skill into your everyday life. Imagine the things you would not do or say because of some unchecked emotion or insecurity. Imagine your ability to act calmly and rationally in the face of external, chaotic circumstances. Imagine flow and calmness as your go-to state of mind. Imagine acting like a leader.

So, if you want to get better at identifying and controlling your emotions so you can be a great leader ... go take an ice bath, find your breath, and lead!

CHAPTER FIVE

Element Two—
Cultural Awareness
and Recognition

THE SECOND ELEMENT OF THE LEADERSHIP PROCESS IS Cultural Awareness and Recognition. For clarity and to be sure we are all speaking the same leadership language, let's define culture. By definition, culture is the "set of shared attitudes, values, goals, and practices that characterizes an institution or organization." Additionally, culture is "the characteristic features of everyday existence shared by a people in a place or time."

In short, and for our purposes, culture is essentially made up of the things we do, not the labels we put on them. Before I explain what I mean by that, let me illustrate how the leadership process is developing up to this point.

Remember our friend Roger, from the Introduction? Once Roger acknowledged his previously unacknowledged emotions, we were able to discuss his situation with some real objectivity and without the shame, fear, and insecurity he was feeling. His newfound self-awareness and vulnerability moved him towards curiosity. He understood that leaders must first be aware of what is happening within themselves before they can move outward and effectively influence what is happening in their environment; in the culture they are building.

I proposed that awareness for leaders was vital and awareness of one's emotions was where we must start for one very simple reason—because emotions drive our actions. Our emotions drive everything we do. And if we are not aware of the very thing that drives our actions, then we are acting without conscious awareness and intention, and we are building an unintentional culture. If that's the case, then we are simply leaving the results of our actions to chance, hope, or assumptions. Chance, hope, or assumption have no place in the leadership equation.

Roger and I then focused on what he was doing, or how he was acting, based on his emotions. "I very often just do the work myself that is not finished, taking too long, or not up to my standards."

"What else?" I prodded.

"I end up giving a laundry list of things to do."

"What's the problem with that?" I asked.

"Now everyone just sits around and waits for me to tell them what to do. Nobody is thinking for themselves or acting with initiative."

About halfway through the week of applying cultural

awareness, Roger called me and shared that he was having some difficulty identifying what his employees actually did, which is a completely normal revelation initially because we are typically not used to this kind of awareness.

He had a staff meeting scheduled for later in the day. I advised him to watch his team during the meeting and to pay attention to how things were being said more than what was being said. I advised him to pay attention to things like tone of voice and body language. For example, were people paying attention or staring into space, or doodling on their notepads?

During our one-on-one meeting a few days later, Roger was dismayed. He felt this way because he saw what his team did for the first time. "We talk past each other and make each other feel small," he told me. "I talk at them, not to them. I overwork the good employees and burn them out. I underwork the ones that need more guidance and that creates resentment among the ones who are shouldering the load. My direction to my people is unclear and haphazard, if I give any direction at all."

At this point I had to stop Roger. I explained that this drill was not so he could beat himself up, but to gain an awareness between the connection of our emotions and the actions they drive. Roger acknowledged that he was not at all conscious of how he was acting, he just seemed to be reacting without intention or forethought. He began to realize that his fear, insecurity, anger, and frustration were driving him to act in ways he was not even aware of, which contributed to a negative culture he had no intention of building.

The moral of the story is that while he was initially dismayed at what he observed after having paid close attention, we could now go about making positive adjustments. But we could only go about making positive adjustments because Roger was now aware of what he and his team did, for better or worse and without judgement. By making informed and positive adjustments, he abated his overall frustrations.

Emotions Drive Culture

In an earlier chapter, we learned that we have between 60,000-70,000 thoughts in one day and 80 to 90% of those thoughts are the same as the day before.[30] For most people, 70% of the time those thoughts are associated with the hormones and emotions of stress: anger, jealousy, frustration, worthlessness, fear, anxiety, insecurity, guilt, envy, etc.[31] [32]

We further learned that every time you have a thought, your brain literally sends a chemical through the body to match how you feel with how you think.[33] [34] This creates a cycle between the mind and body better known as the mind/body connection.

When you begin to feel the way you think, you begin to think the way you feel, the body creates more of those chemicals, and the cycle continues. Unfortunately, the cycle is continuing with the same thoughts over and over, most of which are those associated with the emotions of stress.

To summarize this, if we have the same thoughts based on the same emotions every day, we will take the same actions. If we take the same actions every day, we will have the same experiences every day. We will experience the same workplace culture every day because of those emotionally-driven actions. The same experiences will create the same emotions and we will begin the same, predictable cycle over and over.

Because we are addicted to the emotions and actions of yesterday (and the day before, and the day before that), we will find any event, situation, action, or person to reaffirm our addictive thoughts and behaviors. When we do this enough, when we act a certain way enough based on our established neurochemical addiction, it becomes innate in us. It is now programmed in our subconscious mind and we do it without even thinking about it.

Welcome to what you do. Welcome to your personality. And it is a personality that you are barely aware of. We have become addicted to behaviors we no longer even think about or recognize. We think and behave in a certain way over and over without even realizing it anymore. Positive change can never come unless we at least can recognize the things we do.

Does this Scenario Look Familiar?

Let's say, based on what we've discussed, that you have become addicted to the emotion of anger or frustration. Something happened in your past that made you angry or frustrated and you couldn't let it go, you thought about it over and over. Eventually, you may even forget the details of what happened, but you haven't forgotten the emotion of anger or frustration because you live with it every day.

Since you have now become chemically addicted to the

emotion of anger or frustration and the subsequent actions they drive, but you have forgotten the actual source of your anger or frustration, you need to find a new source somewhere else. That's what addicts do; they find their fix to their addiction wherever they can.

You see your boss do something and you think to yourself, "Look at what that jerk just did! He makes me so angry!" Addiction satisfied. Then you go to your co-worker and tell her what a jerk your boss is and how angry he makes you. But she doesn't feel the same way. She saw what he did, but it didn't make her angry. Then you think to yourself, "I can't believe she isn't mad at what that jerk of a boss did! Doesn't she care? Doesn't she see the injustice? God, she makes me so angry!" Addiction satisfied.

Then you find another co-worker and go through the entire scenario. Except this time your co-worker agrees. Jackpot! Now every day you and your new friend who share the same addiction can feed each other over and over. Anger and frustration now fill the air. Now it's what you do!

But you are not an angry person, right? It's just these people around you doing these stupid things that make you angry. Otherwise you're an awesome, loving, and caring person who doesn't get angry.

Reality tells us a different story, however. To the objective observer, you have acted angry or frustrated for as long as they can remember. At first, they thought it was just your mood. But then it persisted, and they concluded you had a generally angry disposition. Eventually, to the person who has witnessed you for an extended period and for the person who has just met you, this has become your personality. Acting angrily or frustrated is just simply what you do.

What's more, think about the impact on your team or family when you consider the scenario above of the angry or frustrated office worker. Substitute any other emotion for anger or frustration in that scenario and consider the consequences. Or consider a combination of these negative emotions and actions of stress in your team or family: worthlessness, anxiety, jealousy, guilt, shame. What happens if we, as leaders, fail to recognize the consequences of this pattern?

By the time we are 35 years old, 95% of who we are has become a set of memorized behaviors and emotions stored in our subconscious mind.[35] [36] Isn't it worth it as leaders, and as human beings, to begin to take stock of what we do by exercising a little Cultural Awareness and Recognition?

Becoming Aware of Culture

In Element One, Emotional Awareness and Recognition, we showed that emotions drive our actions and if we want to be in control of our actions, we must first be aware of our emotions. Emotions drive our actions and now those very actions we take every day—the things we do—make up our culture.

What do I mean when I say culture is made up of the things we do and not the labels we put on them? Well, it's fine to say we want, or have, a culture of, say, "excellence." There is nothing wrong with putting that label, "excellence," out there.

The problem is too many leaders and organizations stop there and that's unacceptable. If you can't define or articulate the things you do that create excellence, then you don't have a culture of excellence.

Before we do anything, we must identify the things we do that make up our culture. Not what we should do. Not what we want to do, not what we plan to do, but what we actually do. And we must define what we do without judgement, for better or for worse.

So, like in Element One where we focus on awareness and recognition of our emotions, in Element Two we focus on awareness and recognition of what we, and those around us, do, i.e.: our culture. And we do this without judgement, for better or for worse.

The reason we focus on awareness in these first two elements of the leadership process is because we can't make positive change to anything unless we are aware of the things that need changing. To say nothing of the fact that if leadership is anything at all, it is situational awareness: The ability to make good decisions based on full knowledge of what is happening around us.

The Elements of a Good Culture

Let's dive a little deeper into what a good culture looks like. No behavior, good or bad, exists in a bubble. If you exhibit good behavior, it will create positive ripple effects. Not always immediately, but it will. Likewise with poor behavior. Exhibit poor behavior and it will create negative ripple effects.

Let's establish what a strong culture looks like. It will have two distinctive characteristics: It will be sustainable and transferable.

It's sustainable ... it's not lighting in a bottle. It's not the perfect storm of circumstances that come together for an instant that creates momentary nirvana. No, a strong culture sustains you during the bad times and propels you during the good times.

It's transferable ... it doesn't leave the team or organization when a core group of people move on. People leave. But a strong culture transfers to that inevitable turnover from year to year, decade to decade, generation to generation.

There are many examples of good, strong cultures out there in business, athletics, the arts—in all walks of life. I believe I was part of one of those enviable cultures as a Navy SEAL. No culture is without its faults. But the overriding feeling when you walk into a strong culture, one that is sustainable and transferable like the SEAL Teams, is palpable. There is a clear sense of the way things are done and that if you don't get on board fast, you'll likely be left behind.

The SEAL Teams: Sustainable and Transferable

June 6, 1944, or D-Day, was the Allied invasion of Normandy. It was a historical military action that turned the tide of the war in Europe, essentially ridding the world of Adolf Hitler and his quest for world domination. The problem was that the invasion of Normandy was the war's worst kept secret. In preparation for the invasion, the Nazi Army constructed massive steel barriers, laden with explosives, off the shores of Normandy to prohibit the thousands of Allied ships and boats from coming ashore.

A gentleman named Draper Kaufman was tasked with forming a Naval Combat Demolition Unit (later to become the Underwater Demolition Teams (UDT), which still later became the SEAL Teams) to remove these massive barriers and effectively create alleyways for the ships and boats to land on the beaches of Normandy.

After intensive training, these volunteers were each provided a mask, swim fins, a knife, and a satchel of explosives. They were tasked to swim in before the waves of thousands of allied ships and boats, place explosives on the massive steel barriers, and create the needed alleyways for the landing. They would be doing this under the noses of the Nazi Army with essentially a one-way ticket. Their survival after they did their job, destroying the barriers to create the needed alleyways for the landing crafts to go ashore, was left to their own courage and ingenuity.

As such, they sustained a 53% casualty rate with nearly one in five killed.[37] [38] But, they accomplished their mission, the invasion was a success, and the fate of the free world was determined that day. A culture was established that day with a seemingly impossible, some may say suicidal, mission.

Sustainable and transferable …

Let's fast forward to April 2009. Captain Phillips of the Maersk Alabama, a U.S. cargo ship, was taken hostage by Somali Pirates off the coast of Somalia in the Indian Ocean. After a few days of stand-off between the Pirates and the U.S. Navy, it became clear the pirates were going to kill Captain Phillips and there was no clear way to make a rescue attempt.

A plan was concocted to fly in three Navy SEAL Snipers and their spotters sixteen hours and 8,000 miles from Virginia; have them parachute out of an airplane in the dead of night and into the ocean with their small boats and weapons. From there, drive their small boats to a large Navy war ship; set up on the fantail of the Navy war ship, and at the exact moment that the three pirates showed themselves in one of the five small windows of the covered lifeboat the pirates had escaped on with Captain Phillips, the three SEAL Snipers would simultaneously fire their weapons from one moving platform to another, killing the pirates and saving Captain Phillips' life.

That was the plan? Yup, that was the plan. And it is exactly what they did.

Sustainable and transferable. The time between the Normandy alleyway operation to the operation to save Captain Phillips spanned two generations. But that's what culture does. It transcends generations, missions, personalities, and capabilities. The only thing similar between these two Navy SEAL operational examples of culture is the seemingly impossible nature of the missions that were undertaken. The precision of their actions, however, remained constant.

The bottom line on the art of Cultural Awareness and Recognition is simple: figure out what you do, for better or for worse and without judgement. Do this and it will be clear where you need to focus your energy for positive change moving forward. Fail to do it and you will be left in a world of meaningless labels, bad morale, and poor performance.

CHAPTER SIX

Observing Culture, Practicing Awareness ... and Cold Exposure

My Early Exposure to the Culture

Young SEAL trainees are introduced to all sorts of physical, mental, and emotional challenges. I fared pretty well at those challenges at BUD/S training. I could run and swim fast, do a lot of pullups, pushups, and flutter kicks, and didn't particularly mind the cold water.

However, there was one area early on that had my number … the obstacle course.

About half-way or so through the obstacle course my forearms and my grip would get smoked. Then the second half of the obstacle course would become a series of T.V. blooper worthy falls from the obstacles because I simply couldn't hold on to anything.

As that painfully went on for several obstacle course runs, I began to adjust my strategy. I decided to pace myself. Slow down, I told myself, and that would delay the onset of the muscle fatigue in my forearms and grip. My strategy seemed to make things worse.

The first couple of times a trainee goes through the obstacle course at BUD/S there is a little leeway given to them by the instructors. There is a certain amount of technique that needs to be learned so the first time through the course is very much a familiarization run. The second time through the course the trainee is certainly expected to have adjusted to the technique and successfully complete the course. By the third time the expectation is that the trainee completes the course with an acceptable time. I wasn't there yet.

As I couldn't seem to get the hang of the obstacle course, things began to take a turn for the worse. I was beginning to attract the attention of the instructors. They were smelling blood in the water and that's a problem for any SEAL trainee. As my confidence was being shaken every time I stepped onto the obstacle course, the instructors were close by to further demoralize me and attempt to send me on the path of quitting. Such is life at BUD/S training.

One day one of the instructors approached me right before we were set to make another run on the obstacle course. As I was bracing myself for whatever mental, emotional, or physical pain he was about to rain down on me, he asked me a question, "What's the problem?" I provided the standard trainee to instructor responses, "No excuse," "I'll find out," "I suck," whatever. Then he shocked me.

He said, "No, really. Tell me what the problem is. Nobody can figure out why you are so bad at the obstacle course and you need to get it right, fast." I explained the problem with my forearms and grip and told him how I was trying to pace myself to stave off the fatigue. I explained that I was practicing during off hours and just couldn't seem to get it right.

"No!" he shouted at me. "That's lactic acid building up in your muscles. You're giving it time to settle in and wreak havoc on your forearms and grip. It takes about four minutes or so for lactic acid to build up. Be faster than the four minutes. Beat the lactic acid. Attack it, Lt. Doebler. Sitting back gets you nowhere except dead."

I will never forget his response because, among other things, it introduced me fully to the concept of action as the default mode of operation. But it went deeper than that. It's easy to act when things are going well, when everything is lined up for you and confidence is high. It's entirely another thing to take that tact when you feel like you are giving your best, but things keep getting worse, as they seemed to be for me on the obstacle course.

I should have been able to complete, and to be honest excel at, the obstacle course challenge by then. I knew the techniques and was certainly fit enough. I was faced with equal sets of circumstances at play. My choices were to continue to pace myself and sit back, or "act." Like any good SEAL, I refocused myself, said "fuck it," and went for it. The days of obstacle course ineptitude were gone forever.

It's strange—the little things you remember that have impact in your life. And make no mistake, the obstacle course at BUD/S training is a little thing. But I'll never forget it. I'll never forget the wink the instructor gave me as I easily finished the course that day. And most of all, I'll never forget telling myself, "That will never happen again. When I'm not sure, when I can go one way or the other, I will always act."

What Do Navy SEALs Do?

Now let's be careful because there can be a tendency to over-think culture in terms of what we do because we do a lot of things. Don't overthink it. Teams, organizations, families, and yes, ourselves, have consistent behaviors that make up our culture. They do not include the occasional mistake, or occasional good deed, as the case may be. They are the consistent elements of "what we do," for better or for worse and without judgement.

From my perspective as a former Navy SEAL, what did the SEAL Teams do? What was their culture? Well, a couple of things on this; First, we didn't have posters on the wall high-lighting a label we put on what we did. There is nothing wrong with having posters on the wall doing this, we just didn't have them. At least when I was there.

Here is an important point before I go any further; If another SEAL and I listed four things that SEALs do to make up their culture, we may each list four separate behaviors. But I'm confident we would look at each other's list and say, "Yes, that's accurate." Here is my list of the things we did that stood out to me during my time in the SEAL Teams:

The first is that action was the default mode of operation. Given equal scenarios where a decision could be made to act or sit back, we acted.

Next, "yes first." If something was to be done our answer was "yes." We focused on the ways things could be done, not on the reasons something couldn't be done. "Yes first," because there is always a way.

Additionally, we said "yes" because we had big, out-of-the-box ideas. But we executed them inside a disciplined planning process. The plan would tell us why "yes" and how we would overcome obstacles, not be bound by them.

Keep in mind, "yes first" was the spirit in which we operated. You obviously can't say yes to everything every time somebody asks you for something. Our spirit, however, was "yes first." We knew the plan would tell us if it was possible and our ability to effectively prioritize tasks would make it an operational reality.

Finally, we worked unemotionally and methodically. I've never been part of a group that exhibited more passion and enthusiasm for work and life. However, when the time came to work, emotions were checked, and we methodically went about the business of mission accomplishment.

What cultural label do we put on that? Beats me! The important thing is that I can tell you what we did. That was our culture.

How It Translates

Let's take a closer look at how I described the Navy SEAL culture. Is there anything in there that wouldn't work for your organization, team, or family?

Your significant other asks if you can do them a favor and before they even explain what the favor is, you say, "Yes, of course I can do you a favor." "Yes" first.

You are having a big Thanksgiving dinner with family. When the inevitable cleanup starts, instead of asking the obligatory, "Do you need help?" (which you probably don't mean because ... of course they need help!) you simply jump in and act. You wipe down the counter, you take out the garbage, you sweep the floor, whatever it takes. Your default mode of operation is action!

Do these two examples lend themselves to a good family culture? Yes, I think they do! Would they make a good business culture? Again, yes, I think they would!

Focus on Observation Instead of Conclusions

The purpose of this element of the process, Cultural Awareness and Recognition, is just that—awareness and recognition. Focus on conclusions later. For example, you may conclude that you have a culture of respect. That's fine and it may be an accurate conclusion. But the art of Cultural Awareness and Recognition is being able to be specific about the things you do to create respect, which can be a little different for everyone.

What are the specific things you notice that your team does that leads you to conclude you have a culture of respect?

Maybe everyone always says, "please" and "thank you." Perhaps you notice that nobody interrupts the person speaking. Or, when two people begin talking at the same time, they are both willing to defer to the other to speak first. If you were an outsider walking into an environment like this, you would rightly conclude that there is an obvious atmosphere of respect and you would be able to specifically explain why.

Yes, positivity is better than negativity. Science tells us that the negative emotions of stress, anger, anxiety, jealousy, and worthlessness literally down-regulate our genes and make us sick. Likewise, the positive emotions like love, gratitude, abundance, and worthiness upregulate our genes and make us better.[39]

However, when we are looking for areas of improvement, we should focus on the things that we do that cause us to struggle or the things we do where we are successful in spite of them. It's fine to acknowledge the good things we do so we can keep doing them. But to get better, we need to be hyper aware of the bad so we can make honest and meaningful adjustments.

This was the case with Roger, before he made his informed and positive adjustments. When he said, "We talk past each other and make each other feel small," he was mostly drawing a conclusion.

I pressed him by asking him, "How?"

I knew he had done the work when he rattled off several examples of what he observed at the meeting. He noted that when people weren't speaking, they were sitting with their arms crossed and were pushed away from the table; a classic sign of disrespect to those speaking. He observed that any time a junior member of the team would generate an original idea or, heaven forbid, disagree with a more experienced member of the team, the more experienced team member would cite their experience to dismiss their more junior teammate's opinion. He concluded that if the more experienced team member didn't outright disagree using their experience alone as the reason, they would simply roll their eyes and slightly turn away from the junior member of the team who was speaking.

These were very specific behaviors that he had not noticed because he was either not looking for them in the past or they had become such common place he didn't even consider them at all. He summed up what he observed as talking past each other and making each other feel small.

Work Backwards If You Like

We've all been places where we walked into a room and felt a distinct energy, be it positive or negative. Likewise, with people. We've met someone and truly felt an energy. We couldn't explain it, but we felt it. This electromagnetic energy put off by people, or groups of people, is absolutely real.[40]

If you are having a hard time figuring out what people do in order to identify the current culture, work backwards from the energy you feel, especially when it is a negative energy. Once you have this awareness of the energy you feel, seeing what people do to create the energy you feel will be easy.

The negative energy you feel can take many forms or carry many labels. The same drill holds here. Don't simply label.

Identify the things that are being done to create the energy you feel. Then label it if you like.

When you feel a negative energy and you see people interrupting and speaking over each other, moving frantically from task to task, and yelling directions or complaints to no one in particular, you can rightly label this a culture of chaos, for example. But you can only label it because you are aware and recognize what people are doing.

Practicing the Art Through Cold Exposure

Awareness and recognition are skills that need to be practiced in order to sharpen them. Just like each element of the leadership process builds on the one before it, so too does practicing the art of each element through cold exposure.

When we discussed Emotional Awareness and Recognition, we were clear on the fact that every time you step into an ice bath you are going to feel an emotion. To practice the awareness and recognition of your emotions we must consistently expose ourselves to the cold and identify the underlying emotion we feel. When we do this, we come to realize that we can feel many different emotions at the same time, and they can change drastically from day to day. Once you've identified how you feel, next pay attention to what you do before, during, and after the ice bath or other cold exposure.

What are you doing before you jump into the cold shower? Are you pacing around the bathroom looking for something else to do like brush your teeth again or look for those darn nail clippers because you may want to trim your fingernails later this month? Are you spending an extraordinary amount of time on your phone browsing social media only to realize you are now running late...so you'll do the cold part of the shower tomorrow? Did you skip the shower altogether? Did you decide to get the water just a little cold, because you want to allow yourself the opportunity to ease into it?

In other words, did you procrastinate or make excuses to not do the cold exposure at all? Did you procrastinate and make excuses not to do the hard thing?

When you jumped in the cold shower or ice bath, did you make a real show of it? Did you lace your time in the cold with expletives, "Oh fuck, oh shit, oh fuck, oh shit!" or some other overly-dramatic form of expression to signify how terrible it all is for you? Did you forgo any real effort to find your breath and relax and just go directly to bracing all your muscles, gritting your teeth, and clenching your jaw to survive?

When you exited the cold, did you run for a towel or a robe immediately and hunker down into survival mode until you started to warm up a little? Did you make a point to tell the first person who would listen how dramatic your cold exposure experience was?

It may sound like I'm being overly-critical if you did some or all the things I'm describing. Be rest assured, I'm not criticizing or judging in any way. I listed these possible actions because they are typical. The point here is to be aware of them. Why is it important to be aware of what we do before, during, and after cold exposure? Because it is likely a mirror into what you do during stress in your daily life.

So, if you are having trouble figuring out what you do during your day to identify your culture, this cold exposure drill will help you be more aware. Again, it is an intellectual drill to help you become more aware in a safe learning environment. Once we figure out what we actually do, we can then begin to decide what we want to do, or how we want to behave (coming soon in the next element, Guidelines For Behavior!)

In short, if you want to practice the art of Cultural Awareness and Recognition, get into an ice bath or cold shower and identify what you do, for better or worse, without judgement!

This element of the leadership process allows us to see how things actually are, without judgement, for better or for worse. Without this realization we cannot make targeted, necessary, and effective change. Without this realization we cannot make the kind of change or adjustments that leaders make because leaders first see things for how they are, not how they want them to be (that comes next!).

CHAPTER SEVEN

Managing the Extremes and the In-betweens—Being in the Moment

B Y 2017, I HAD LEFT THE FBI AND STARTED MY LEADERSHIP consulting firm, Leader 193. I arrived at a client meeting in the City of brotherly love (Philadelphia) a little early, so I tucked into a coffee shop to kill some time and read a book by Simon Sinek called, *Leaders Eat Last.*

The book began with a story of a pilot whose nickname was Johnny Bravo. In the story, Johnny Bravo was providing air support for a Special Operations Unit patrolling in Afghanistan. As the story moves along, Johnny Bravo describes how the unit he was supporting patrolled into a narrow canyon that left them dangerously exposed to all manner of enemy aggression. What's more, a fog had settled over the top of the canyon, which obstructed Johnny Bravo's view of the patrol and his ability to properly support them from his aircraft.

As Johnny Bravo deftly maneuvered his aircraft underneath the fog over the canyon to get a better view of the patrol, he realized he was witnessing the patrol in a gun fight. They had been ambushed. From there, I was enthralled with Johnny Bravo's ability and bravery as he maneuvered underneath the clouds inside the narrow canyon to provide fire support for the Special Operators fighting for their lives on the ground.

I was immersed in the story. First of all, how can you not love a story about somebody nicknamed Johnny Bravo? But mostly I was enjoying the story because it was familiar to me. I recognized all the elements of this story on a personal level. Patrolling with a Special Operations Unit into a dangerously exposed area. The vision of the high walls of a mountainous canyon that offer an enemy combatant the perfect vantage point to wreak havoc on a patrol. Ambushes, fire fights, and the presence of a night fog in enemy territory.

I was engrossed! The writing was beautiful and the story inspiring. Until I was snapped out of my trance by my hands shaking and sweat pouring off my face onto the pages of the book. I was in the throes of a panic attack in the middle of a city coffee shop packed with customers on their way to work.

We'll come back to this ...

The Science of Being in the Moment:
You Don't Have to Be a Hippie

As we've discussed, awareness and recognition are skills. As such, they are skills that need to be practiced and honed. We've discussed practicing the art of awareness and recognition through cold exposure and the science behind the emotional and cultural aspects of awareness and recognition. What we need to touch on now is the skill that allows you to practice the skills of awareness and recognition—being in the moment.

In the West, the notion of being in the moment has long been associated with "woo-woo, hippie propaganda," monks, weirdos, and other human outliers who spend their time sitting around not contributing to society and too afraid or lazy to join the daily grind, better known as the rat race.

This notion is the very reason why I include so much science in this process of leadership. It allows the cynics to see the importance of being in the present moment without feeling like they are being manipulated into a cult. The believers of this notion don't really need the science because they have experienced the power that being in the moment brings, but they enjoy the science because it helps them understand why they feel the way they feel when they are in the moment.

Combining the belief of the importance of being in the moment and the science behind it allows both groups, the cynics and the believers, to meet gently in the middle and find a blissful coherence and an understanding of the other's point of view.

In cognitive neuroscience terms, being in the moment is referred to as metacognition. Metacognition is essentially an awareness, thinking about what you are thinking about, having a feeling about what you are feeling, being aware of your awareness.[41] If the feeling you are feeling is born of some spontaneous, high energy event, like hitting a patch of ice when you are driving, it will likely automatically trigger an action, mental or physical.

This is the case with intense emotions. We all generally recognize when we are extremely angry, frightened, sad, or happy. We may not, however, be aware of the actions these extreme emotions drive, like slamming on the brakes when we hit that patch of ice. The key, for our purposes, is to practice metacognition at all times, not just on the extremes, because life is generally happening between the extremes.

The Basic Effects of Being in the Moment or Practicing Metacognition

The more you observe, the more you can change. It's a simple truth. Have you ever seen yourself on a recording and thought, "My God, do I really act that way?" Perhaps you were record-ed at a party after a few cocktails. You may think, "Next time I'll stop after two!" Perhaps the wedding videographer caught you on the dance floor at your best friend's wedding. You may think, "I need to take that move out of my dance rotation." Maybe you saw how you reacted at your child's sporting event after your spouse recorded it and thought, "Maybe next time I won't scream inane corrections to my daughter and embarrass her (and myself) in front of everyone."

You would absolutely change many of your behaviors if you could only see yourself in action. Well, we can see our-selves in action by practicing metacognition or, being in the moment.

If You Are Not Present, Then You Are Somewhere Else

We've spent a lot of time discussing emotions. Emotions are simply a record of the past.[42] [43] We've discussed that we spend an inordinate amount of time on our negative emotions of the past and, as such, we've become neurochemically addicted to them.

Because of this addiction, we are bringing the past into the present. Even right now, we are likely focused on an emotion triggered by some past event. And because of this, we now extrapolate that emotion into the future. We already know how we are going to feel in the future because we are bringing it forward from our past emotions. In other words, we're thinking something along the lines of, "Well, I'd better prepare myself to feel this way later today and tomorrow because that person or thing made me feel this way last week and yesterday."

Don't confuse recognizing the things you have to do tomorrow with how you are setting yourself up to feel tomorrow. These are two different conversations and we now know that how you feel will dictate the way you will "do." Will you be present, in the moment and completing your tasks from a place of enthusiasm, confidence, giving, love, and gratitude? Or will you complete the task from a place of past anger, jealousy, resentment, frustration, and worthlessness? The distinction is clear, and it matters. Especially in leadership!

This concept seems simple when you read it. But let's not assume or hope we are aware of it all the time because science tells us we are not. In fact, science tells us we are the opposite of "in the moment" most of the time. If you are not in the present moment, you are somewhere else. That somewhere else is in the past you've become addicted to and the future you've become addicted to based on the past you can't let go of. This is a scary proposition if you think about it.

Do One Thing Well, or Two Things Poorly

As a former Navy SEAL, FBI Special Agent, and SWAT operator, I've fired countless rounds of ammunition from weapons. That type of repetition produces a certain amount of muscle memory to be sure, which is not necessarily a bad thing. But does an established muscle memory mean I can stop concentrating, or being in the moment, for each step of the process of, say, reloading my weapon? Let's break it down.

Here are, in general, the steps one takes when reloading their handgun. If you are not a gun person, stay with me, you'll eventually get where I'm going with this analogy:

1. Upon recognizing my weapon has run out of bullets, or "gone dry," I turn my weapon 90 degrees, keeping it at face level.

2. I locate the magazine release button. (The "magazine" is the thing that holds the bullets and is held inside the handle of the weapon, aka "magazine well.")

3. I press the magazine release button.

4. I watch the magazine fall from the magazine well.

5. I grab my spare magazine from my hip, and I watch it as I place it into the magazine well while keeping my weapon at face level.

6. I press the slide release and watch the slide move forward, thereby chambering the round (bullet) and making it ready to fire.

7. I properly re-grip my weapon.

8. As I point the weapon back at my target, I acquire my front sights.

9. I place the fat part of the tip of my finger on the trigger.

10. I begin to squeeze the slack out of the trigger.

11. I properly identify my target.

12. I pull the rest of the slack out of the trigger and fire.

13. I immediately re-acquire my front sight and determine if I need to fire again.

This process takes probably 2-3 seconds for a seasoned shooter. Despite the speed with which this magazine change can be performed, the fact remains that these are all separate and distinct actions. Because these are separate and distinct actions, each action requires the shooter's full attention to do it correctly. In other words, the shooter must be fully in the moment for each action to ensure the action is completed successfully.

Even the best shooters get lazy and begin to rely solely on muscle memory alone for this process. It's understandable. In fact, the experienced shooter who relies on muscle memory may successfully complete this sequence of events to re-load their weapon 999 times out of 1000. These are pretty good odds!

But what happens when that one time you don't successfully re-load is when you are in an actual gun fight and not on the range practicing? Does 999 out of 1000 sound good now?

Nope, not so much. You are now 0 for 1 and have increased your chances of getting killed exponentially. Your strategy at this point is to hope your opponent isn't good enough to take advantage of your mishap and shoot you dead.

As leaders, we don't like hope as a strategy. As leaders, we simply prefer to get it right.

The point is simple: why would you rely on muscle memory and risk getting it wrong one time when you can be assured you will get it right every time by being in the moment for each separate and distinct action?

One of the best firearms instructors I've ever had says, "There is no such thing as multitasking. You can either do one thing really well or two things poorly." If it is important enough to be in the moment on the battlefield when your life literally depends on it, then it is certainly worth considering during our day-to-day activities and interactions.

When we move from task to task to task our brain moves into a state of incoherence that triggers our fight or flight response, or our Sympathetic Nervous System.[44] [45] The Sympathetic Nervous System helps us in times of crisis to focus our energy. For example, if we were being chased by a Grizzly Bear, our Sympathetic Nervous System focuses our attention on survival: fight, flight, or hide. We don't need to be thinking of anything else in this instance other than survival. All our natural bodily functions move their energy to our limbs to enhance our ability to run or otherwise survive. In instances like this, this is a good thing!

However, when we "multitask" all day every day, we unnecessarily put our brain in a state of incoherence. We unnecessarily activate the fight or flight response of our Autonomic Nervous System. We unnecessarily narrow our focus on only what is right in front of our noses. We unnecessarily move energy from our core bodily functions (like digestion, circulation, and reproductive systems) to our extremities. And, as we've learned, it becomes the behavior we are addicted to. When we are constantly in a state of fight or flight, like we are when we constantly move our focus and attention, our body moves to a state of "dis-ease."[46] [47] Yes, we become sick, worn down, anxious, and otherwise moody and irritable. Not exactly great leadership traits.

Conversely, when our brain is focused on one thing at a time, it relaxes and activates the rest and digestion, or Parasympathetic Nervous System. When our brain is relaxed, we view our surroundings from a wider lens. We can consider possibilities and create new opportunities. Internally, our autonomic systems (digestion, blood flow, reproductive systems, organ function) are operating normally[48] [49] and not unnecessarily stressing the body or sending it into "dis-ease."[50] [51] We are healthier, stronger, happier, and clearer-headed because we are not letting the emotions of stress dominate our being. Don't these traits feel more aligned with great leadership?

Consider the effects of the interactions you have as a leader when your brain is relaxed and open to every consideration. Consider the quality of your decisions when you can see the entire picture, not just what is in front of your nose for the short time you are considering options.

Now Extrapolate the Principle Out to
Your Personal Life

My premise is that these principles needed for battlefield success are transferable to every part of your life, both personally and professionally. Have you ever had a disagreement with your significant other because you weren't paying attention? Do you have those confrontations when you are truly listening to what is being said and responding with thought and measure? No, not likely. Now think back to the times you have been in your boss' office or at a co-worker's desk. Remember when they were talking to you and at the same time immersing themselves in their e-mail or something else on their computer that had nothing to do with you. How did that make you feel? Less than significant I imagine. And if it didn't make you feel less than significant it's because you have been conditioned to accept this behavior as normal and acceptable.

Too often, those in leadership positions feel they have the right to multitask when someone is speaking to them. Maybe, as the boss, you believe you are hearing everything that is being said to you. Maybe you are giving good direction based on what you heard (or thought you heard), or maybe you are not. Because you have chosen to not be in the moment in the conversation, you can't say for sure if you've missed anything. Perhaps you are hearing the words, but are you missing the non-verbal cues that so often tell us more about what is happening than the words themselves? Now you will make a leadership decision based on incomplete information. You are not situationally aware, or in the moment, and therefore the odds of your decision being a good decision have been left to chance.

When we are in the moment with our conversations, we can recognize our own emotions and ensure our response is based on conscious thought, not on emotion. Having an emotional response is just like using muscle memory to change your weapon's magazine; you are relying on hope to ensure it works.

Remember, we are talking about getting the interaction right by being in the moment. If we get the interaction right, then we are in a position to make the best decision because it will be a conscious decision based on a full knowledge of all the information at hand. We may get the decision wrong, but that's ok because we will have been fully aware of our thought process and can then make adjustments going forward.

Breathing and Cold Exposure to Practice the Art of Being in the Moment

When I conduct breathing and cold exposure seminars, I always ask the participants beforehand who has tried to meditate and who simply can't seem to get it right. Overwhelmingly, those who have tried to meditate acknowledge they can't seem to do it. The reason for this is because people have a misconception about what meditation is.

In the Tibetan language, meditation means to become familiar with your mind.[52] [53] That's it! It's no different than emotional awareness and recognition or metacognition. To be familiar with your mind you must be present and in the moment to where your mind is right now. We can practice this through some basic breathing and meditative work.

Maybe someday I'll write the Leader 193 handbook for meditation, but not today. I simply want to provide you a few basic guidelines using breathing/meditation and cold exposure to practice the art of being in the moment. This will allow you to master the elements of the leadership process.

Start your meditation for about five minutes (you can set an alarm if you need to). You want to focus on ONE THING. For our purposes, let's focus on your breath. It does not matter for now if you are sitting, standing, or lying down; just be comfortable. Inhale through your nose, not your mouth. I recommend exhaling through your nose as well, but if you prefer to start exhaling through your mouth that is fine. Eventually you'll want to do full nasal breathing.

As you begin your breathing, your focus is to remain only on your breath. When your mind wanders to something else, bring it back to your breath. It does not matter how many times your mind wanders. As long as you are familiar with your mind you can bring your attention back to your breath every time. If your mind wanders fifty times in one minute of breathing and you bring it back to your breath every time ... congratulations! You are meditating. It's as simple as that.

What can you expect during the early stages of your breathing/meditation practice? Frustration for starters. You will be shocked at how hard it is to sit for five minutes and focus your attention. You won't believe how many times your mind wanders. You will feel like you spent only .01% of the time focusing on your breath and the rest of the time bringing your mind back from where it wandered. Good! You're meditating. You are aware of where your mind is, and you are consciously bringing it back to where you want it. Like anything else, it will take time to get good at. You must put in the work. When your body is screaming to get up and get on with your day, which it will, you must force yourself to sit still and focus on your breath. When your mind wanders, bring it back. Eventually you will learn to focus on your breath to such a degree that you will finally get past your analytical mind and into your subconscious mind, which is where all of our creation and peace comes from when we consciously tap into it.

For now, though, start with focusing on your breath for five minutes a day and when your mind wanders, bring it back. When you do this you practice being in the moment. When you learn how to be in the moment you will have emotional and cultural awareness. When you have emotional and cultural awareness you can make a true and honest assessment of the areas needed for improvement. When you practice being in the moment, you will have full situational awareness and be able to make good leadership decisions based on all the information at hand.

The Cold Too?

Yes, the cold too. Cold exposure takes your ability to focus on your breath and learn to be in the moment to the next level because there is no hiding or lying in an ice bath or cold shower.

The goal is not to endure the cold. The goal is to remain calm in the cold. Anyone can grit their way through it. But leaders remain calm amidst the chaos and use grit only when they need it, which is not as often as we think.

Remember, science tells us that the brain relaxes when it is present, in the moment, and focused on one thing at time. Not when it is scattered from thing to thing to thing. Think about where your mind scatters to when you step into an ice bath or cold shower. "This sucks! How much longer? Why am I doing this? This is so cold? I want to get out!" When we think this way, we have no coherence in the brain because it is scattered. Thus, we will not focus our attention on one thing and remain calm.

But when we focus on one thing in the cold—our breath—we know that our brain relaxes. We know that when we consciously exhale, we activate the vagus nerve which serves to calm us down.[54] [55] In the cold is where you test your ability to practice your breathing and meditation focus because if you don't, you will not do well. You will feel panicked, uncertain, and out of control. Again, not traits of a good leader.

However, if you move your practice of breathing and meditation to the cold you will thrive in the chaos and prove to yourself you can do it under any circumstance. When your mind wanders in an ice bath, which it will, bring it back to your breath. Every time. Be conscious of where your mind is and bring it back when it wanders, and you will find calm and consciousness in the chaos of the cold.

Will it be easy? No! That is why we must put in the work. It is why when we put in the work, we develop a unique and enviable skill that separates leaders from everyone else.

Breathe, meditate, get cold, and learn to be in the moment!

How Did That Coffee Shop Story End?

As you recall, I left you with me reading and enjoying my book in the coffee shop only to suddenly realize my hands were shaking and I was sweating profusely. The coffee shop was packed, and I was sure I was about to draw attention to myself if I hadn't already. So, what to do?

First, I recognized what was happening. I was in the moment and recognized that some extreme emotion had been triggered by reading the war chronicles of Johnny Bravo. I had Emotional Awareness and Recognition because I was in the moment and present to how I was feeling.

Next, I recognized what I was doing. Again—a form of Cultural Awareness and Recognition based on the concept of being in the moment, or metacognition, or meditation. I was having a panic attack! When I realized I was having a panic attack I sort of double-dipped because I started to panic about having a panic attack. I was in a moment of chaos to say the least. So, I followed a familiar process because I realized I had been here before. When? Every time I stepped into an ice bath.

The sympathetic, or fight or flight, response you get when you enter an ice bath is nothing more than a panic attack. Then I reminded myself what I customarily do when I get into an ice bath—I focus on my breath. I remembered that focusing on one thing calms the brain. I remembered that when I exhale it activates the vagus nerve, which will serve to calm me down.[56]

And I remembered that I have done this hundreds of times before in an ice bath so this should not be any different.

And that is exactly what I did. I focused on my breath and only my breath. Not on the noise of my hands shaking, sweating profusely, or how silly I might have looked sitting at the coffee shop table. None of those things were going to help me. I breathed deeply in through my nose and exhaled gently through my mouth. By my second breath I was calm. I had stopped shaking and sweating and was calm and in full control of my mind and body, just like when I get into an ice bath. Just like when I practice my breathing and meditation.

I went on to have a successful meeting and when I arrived home I shared what happened with my wife. She asked if I needed to go see someone. Was I suffering from PTSD? I was not and am not ever opposed to seeing a professional regarding this or any other struggle I may be having. However, I opined to my wife that the only thing a professional would do is try to help me get past the panic attack and I already know how to do that. She agreed. Even worse, they may try to prescribe me some sort of medication to "help" my condition. We both knew this was not a road I should go down because masking the symptoms of the panic does nothing to fix the problem. And, again, I had already shown a full understanding of what happened and how to positively deal with it. We agreed to watch it for the time being.

I have not had a panic attack since.

Imagine all the people who suffer from some form of PTSD, anxiety, depression, or panic attacks to one degree or another. Think about the havoc it wreaks on their lives. Think about the power they are giving away to narcotics, prescribed or otherwise, that is taking away the power to heal themselves.

This is a true story. My hope in sharing it with you is to show how this leadership process allows you to thrive in chaotic environments and improve your life based on the simple concept of learning how to be in the moment, understanding how you are feeling, and what actions those feelings drive.

CHAPTER EIGHT

Element Three— Guidelines for Behavior

M OST PEOPLE CAN AGREE THAT BEING A NAVY SEAL AND an FBI Special Agent are two exciting jobs. But one of my favorite jobs was the one I held after I left the SEAL Teams and before I entered the FBI: selling copiers. I took the job because, like most people who take a job, I needed a paycheck. I left the SEAL Teams after an injury that cut my career short. I had every intention of staying in the Navy as a SEAL, but it wasn't to be. I got into sales on the recommendation of a friend. The same friend recommended copier sales as a start because, as he put it, "It's the Vietnam of sales. If you can sell a copier you can sell anything. Plus, they'll take anybody."

Not surprisingly, I was not excited about this job at first. I played all the typical mind tricks to convince myself I was adding value to society, that my job mattered now as it had before. I was losing that battle. I never did, and never will, care about copiers.

What I found that I loved, however, was the environment the leader created. The environment was safe because it was predictable. Because the environment was safe and predictable, I enjoyed going to work. Because I enjoyed going to work, I did good work. WE did good work. Our team always outperformed other sales teams throughout the country. Not because we loved copiers. It was because we loved the environment. And because we loved the safe and predictable environment, and because the safe and predictable environment created social and professional successes, we all had a certain pride working for our copier company.

It was not a great environment because our team enjoyed happy hours and other fun events outside of work. We enjoyed happy hours and other fun events outside of work because we all treated each other with courtesy and respect in the workplace. We treated each other with courtesy and respect in the workplace because certain Guidelines for Behavior were put in place by our leader that he consistently reiterated and enforced.

We felt the kind of pride that so many leaders want from their people out of the gate. Leaders cannot will their people to have pride. They can, however, create the environment that will ultimately lead to the pride leaders desperately want from their team.

By now you are seeing the progression of the elements of the leadership process and how they build upon each other.

Good leadership always starts from the inside and works its way out. As such, we began with Emotional Awareness and Recognition because emotions drive our actions and we must be hyper-focused on our emotions in order to have control over our actions.

As culture is nothing more than the sum of the things we do (which are driven by our emotions) we must have a clear understanding of what our current culture is by practicing Cultural Awareness and Recognition. Only when we are aware of our current culture, for better or worse and without judgement, can we begin the process of defining what we want our culture to be.

Guidelines for Behavior is where the proverbial rubber meets the road. Since actions make up our culture, Guidelines for Behavior now let us begin to define what actions to take so *we* can define our culture, as opposed to letting unchecked emotions define our actions, and hence our culture. Every person, family, and team have a culture. The question is whether you've defined what it is. By definition, a guideline is:

1. A line by which one is guided, such as a cord or rope, to aid a passer over a difficult point or to permit retracing a course

2. An indication or outline of policy or conduct

As the definition shows, having an outline of conduct, or behaviors, serves to set us on our desired path and establish a place to return when we inevitably go off course, because we all venture off course occasionally. Guidelines for Behavior remind us where to go when we have to ask ourselves, "How did we get here? How did things get this crazy?" It will be a deviation from behavior that gets us off course, not some market-specific event.

Remember how we described a good culture? A good culture will propel you during the good times and sustain you during the bad times. Culture is made up of the things you do and how you behave. Therefore, Guidelines for Behavior is the first thing you should check if you or your team has ventured off course.

Behavioral guidelines establish our desired behaviors that make up our culture and set clear expectations. If we expect people to act in a certain way, we need to be clear what that way is. Otherwise, we work on assumptions and hope. We assume somebody knows what to do or how to act; we hope somebody knows what to do or how to act without you, the leader, making it clear for them. Assumptions and hope have no place in the leadership equation. Clear and unambiguous Guidelines for Behavior do.

Who Establishes Guidelines for Behavior and Why?

Who should establish the guidelines? The leader establishes the guidelines because absent clear guidelines people will behave as they choose, for better or worse. It's your team. You are answerable, or accountable, for its performance. Therefore, you establish the parameters for its success.

This is not dictatorial by any stretch of the imagination. We are not asking people to not be themselves. Unless, of course, "yourself" is someone who exhibits rude, anti-social, or destructive behavior that will have an adverse effect on a team or environment. If this is the case, and we have established clear Guidelines for Behavior that people can't or won't abide by, then we can say with clarity and good for all sides, "You are not a cultural fit." Because, again, culture is nothing more than the things you do.

Leaders too often obsess over why people don't love or care about their job more. My guidance is always for them to stop worrying about what people think about the job and focus on creating an *environment* people can love. What environment will people grow to love, or at least respect? One with behavioral predictability. If people are confident they will be treated in a way that is consistent and predictable, they will generally enjoy going to work because of the predictability the environment creates. Once people begin to enjoy the environment, they will begin to have more affinity for the organization and the work, not the other way around.

Just as a reminder that the leadership process is applicable in all aspects of your life, take this premise home, literally. When we exhibit predictable behaviors as spouses, parents, siblings, and friends, our home becomes the place we want it to be. A place of safety and comfort. Not because we say it will be that way, but because of the behaviors we exhibit. And to ensure which behaviors will create the predictability, safety, and comfort we desire at home we need to define them so we can hold each other accountable to them.

Don't confuse environmental predictability with a job that

is inherently unpredictable. Sometimes sales can be unpredictable. Finance can be unpredictable. Being a SEAL and FBI Special Agent can be unpredictable. Being a parent or spouse can be unpredictable. What I'm talking about is the behavioral environment. If the leader expects one thing out of you today, and a different thing tomorrow ... that's an unpredictable environment people will grow tired of. If the leader treats you one way today and another way tomorrow ... that's an unpredictable environment people will grow tired of. If teammates can vent, criticize, and demean at the whim of their emotions without having to answer to the leader for their behavior ... that's an unpredictable environment people will grow tired of.

It's a hard truth that, for many, a job can be nothing more than a means to a financial end. People need to make money; therefore, they need a job. The need to provide for themselves or their family greatly supersedes their need to love their work. There is nothing wrong with this motivation. By and large, the leader should not care about someone's motivation because they have no control over that. What a leader has total control over is the state of the work environment.

Establishing the Right Guidelines

So how do we establish the right Guidelines for Behavior that will define our culture, both as a team and as an individual? Remember, our drill at the end of Culture Awareness and Recognition was to be observant of the behaviors of yourself, your team, your family, and your surroundings. This drill enabled us to identify what our culture is, for better or worse. After we've gone about the business of identifying the reality of our culture, we then must begin to decide what we want it to be ... if different than what it currently is. We begin that process by asking a simple question: *If we didn't change the way we made, marketed, or sold our widget, but behaved in **these** ways, would we get better?*

Your "widget" is your actual job description. Your widget can be war, criminal investigations, selling copiers, being a parent or spouse, care-giving, trading on the stock market, or making deli sandwiches. It doesn't matter what your job title is. How you behave, however, is a different matter altogether and is the thing that will define your culture.

You may be thinking to yourself that your team already has a culture established. Maybe you believe you have established a culture of *trust*. Or maybe the culture you believe you have established is one of *excellence*. You may or may not be right. I can't know if you are right until I hear from you *how* you have established trust or excellence. What are the things you and your team *do* that create trust and excellence? You see, trust and excellence are merely by-products of what you do. They are the label you put on the result of the things you do and how you behave.

For example, imagine you were to approach me and tell me that I need to trust you because we will now trust each other to create a safe and predictable environment. My response may be, very reasonably, that I *don't* trust you. What's more, you can't simply make me trust you by telling me to trust you. Your reply may be something to the effect of, "Why don't you trust me?" My answer will likely consist of a list of the things that you *do* that make me not trust you. Now, as a leader, you must go about the business of *doing* certain things, or *stop doing* certain things, to create the trust you want from me.

The same holds true for defining your culture with terms like "excellence." Please don't misunderstand, there is nothing wrong with saying things like, "We have a culture of excellence." My point is simply that most leaders who say this begin and end there. My question, again, will be *how* are you excellent? Excellence is the byproduct of what you do, how you behave.

Let's break it down more simply. I ask, "Do you trust that person?"

You answer, "Yes."

I respond, "Why?"

You reply, "Because they pay attention when I talk to them. They always do what they say they are going to do. I can always count on them to tell me the truth."

Once again, I comment, "Your team's performance was excellent. I want that for my team. How did you do that?"

You answer, "We always plan before we act. We always finish what we start before moving on to other projects. We do not tolerate gossip or bad mouthing. We do not make emotional decisions. Because we behave in these ways, we achieve excellence."

Using the Leadership Data

As we begin to understand how to establish good Guidelines for Behavior, let's talk about data. Leadership has long been thought of as the intangible behavior; one where leadership training can't really produce a definable return on investment. You may be surprised to learn that leadership studies have been around for some time. It's been my experience that organizations talk a big game on leadership, but then use the excuse of return on investment, or the inability to track return on investment, as the excuse not to invest in leadership training. And the investment I'm talking about is time, not money. Money is the excuse, but time is really the thing organizations don't want to commit to. And a commitment to time is what will ultimately bring the behavioral leadership change everyone is looking for.

There are enough studies to know that the financial cost of bad leadership can be crippling. For example, research conducted by the Blanchard Company shows that less-than-optimal leadership practices cost the typical organization an amount equal to as much as 7% of their total annual sales.[57] Sibson and Company estimate that employee turnover can result in a 16%-50% cost as a percent of industry earnings.[58] The Saratoga Institute estimates that between 9% and 32% of that cost is directly attributable to poor management practices.[59] Meanwhile the Blanchard Company estimates 30% of annual salary to replace a lower skilled, entry-level employee, to as much as 250% of annual salary to replace a highly specialized or difficult-to-replace position.[60] For its part, the Saratoga Institute uses a 100% replacement cost for its calculations.[61]

It's not hard to understand that people leave their jobs because of bad leadership and it costs a lot of money to replace them. It simply begs the question of what to do about it. How do organizations fix this problem? The studies of what makes great teams give us the answer, or at least the start of the answer. A client of mine did an analysis of the financial output of employees who participated in consistent leadership training vs. those who did not. The financial results of those who participated were significantly better than those who did not.

There have been a number of unrelated studies since the 1990s that have focused on what makes a great team. Among them: In 1995, David Lyle (et al), "Leadership, Cohesion, and Team Norms Regarding Cheating and Aggression"; in 1999, Amy Edmundson, "Psychological Safety and Learning Behavior in Work Teams"; in 2010, Anita Williams Wooley (et al), "Evidence for a Collective Intelligence Factor in the Performance of Human Groups"; and Google's "Project Aristotle" in 2015.[62] The key take-away from all of these studies, at least from my perspective, was that great teams were established because of *how* they functioned, not *who* was on them.[63] Furthermore, the *how* was made up of behaviors, not things like having a to-do list, intelligence, or love of a job. And finally, the *how* needed to be established and enforced by the *leader*.[64]

So, since some very committed people went about the work of validating that behaviors make great teams and these behaviors are established and enforced by the leader, let's do them the courtesy of starting the discussion of what makes a good guideline for behavior with some of the studies' conclusions. But first, remember: *If we didn't change the way we made, marketed, or sold our widget, but behaved in **these** ways, would we get better?*

There are surprisingly only a couple of consistent behaviors that successful teams exhibit:

1. Everyone feels like they can speak up and teammates speak in roughly the same proportion. Honest discussion can occur without fear of retribution or insult.

2. Teammates are sensitive to each other's emotions and needs. [65]

In one of the studies, these behaviors were labeled "The Psychological Safe Zone."[66] According to the data, behave in these ways and you will have a successful team. So, as you begin to understand the concept of Guidelines for Behavior inside the leadership process, and search for where to start defining them for your team, family, or organization, perhaps the Psychological Safe Zone is a good place to begin.

I recognize I just summarized years' worth of studies in a few paragraphs. The goal of citing the studies is not to fully break them down. That's been done and I encourage you to go read the studies yourself. The goal is to show how Guidelines for Behavior are the key to establishing a culture you can hold your team or organization accountable to. Behave in these ways and we will get better!

Breaking Down the Behaviors in the Psychological Safe Zone

Let's briefly break down why the behaviors in the Psychological Safe Zone will make your team better if the leader establishes them and enforces them, if it's not already painfully obvious to you. And recognize that these behaviors have nothing to do with your *widget*.

Everyone feels like they can speak up and teammates speak in roughly the same proportion. Honest discussion can occur without fear of retribution or insult. People don't speak up for many reasons. Shyness or a general fear of speaking up in a group are common reasons. This is where *teammates speak in roughly the same proportion* comes in.

Studies show that in a typical four-person group, two people will do 62% of the talking. In a six-person group, three people will do 70% of the talking; and in an eight-person group, three people will do 70% of the talking.[67] We all know these people. Perhaps you are that person? In any event, when we allow for so few people to dominate so much of a conversation, we are only getting the views, opinions, and ideas of those few people. Over time, people generally are not interested in fighting for speaking time in a meeting. It eventually will come down to an attitude of "just get me through this meeting so I can get out of here with some sanity."

People will *feel* like they can speak up when speaking up is a behavioral guideline. When people speak up new ideas are generated and old ways of doing things are tweaked, adjusted, or thrown out. When people speak up, they feel like their opinion matters and they have more skin in the conversation because ... they spoke up. And, as it turns out according to one study cited, it seems people don't necessarily care too much if their idea is used. They just want to know it was heard.[68]

How do we stop two or three people from dominating

60-70% of the conversation? Because you, the leader, have established that *teammates speak in roughly the same proportion*; you, as the leader, get to respectfully enforce this guideline by politely interrupting your conversation hog by saying, "Bill, I'm sorry to interrupt you. Thank you for your input, but you know how we do business around here. We've only got an hour and we need to hear from everyone. So, Jane, please weigh in on ..."

Remember from the Cultural Awareness and Recognition chapter, if you can "reprimand" by saying "that's not how we do business around here" and everyone understands, then you've established a good culture. In this case, *everyone feels like they can speak up* because it is how you do business. It is a behavioral guideline that represents how you do business. Because it's how you act, it is now a part of your culture.

Your conversation hog will never like it because, well, they are a conversation hog. But they will understand it and live by it because you, the leader, have established it and enforced the guideline.

Honest discussion can occur without fear of retribution or insult. This is the other reason people don't speak up. Because they don't feel like having people roll their eyes at them, or talk behind their back, or snicker at them when they present an idea or an opinion. To form, it will probably be your conversation hog that does the eye rolling, gossiping, or snickering when they don't have the floor. The leader's enforcement behind this one takes a little more courage, but if it's a behavioral guideline that makes us better, then it needs to be enforced.

A Quick Thought on Enforcement

How a leader enforces a guideline, especially one like this, comes down to personal style, or your ART. My personal style is very direct. I would probably address an eye roll or snicker in this way, "Ted, why are you rolling your eyes? That is not the way we do business around here. Let me remind everyone before we move on how we behave. We operate in a Psychological Safe Zone, which means that people are free to talk without fear of retribution or insult. Any questions on that? Good. Phillip, please continue."

I hold Ted accountable by asking him why he rolled his eyes. He may or may not have a good answer. It doesn't matter because he was asked the question, and this confirms to my employees how we are doing business. The rest is a simple reminder to everyone of how important this guideline is to me. If the negative behavior continues and Ted has nothing but bad answers after he's asked why, or held accountable, then we move to the consequence phase.

Is my way the correct way to handle this? Beats me. But it is how I would handle it. You may handle it with more subtlety, with a softer touch. Good! The bottom line is that, however you would handle the situation, it should convey that this is not how "we do business here." We behave in *these* ways!

There is no sugar-coating it, confrontation is difficult and will take many of you far outside your comfort zone. Unfortunately, it is a necessary evil because if you don't enforce this guideline, then it is no longer a guideline. It will become a behavior you tolerate, and it is that behavior that will define your team and you as a leader.

Emotional Sensitivity to Needs and Emotions

Teammates must be sensitive to each other's emotions and needs. My intention for this book is for it to be a very clear and raw guide on the Process, Art, and Science of Leadership; a user's manual, if you will. There are many stories behind the basis for my philosophies and leadership process. But, as you have hopefully seen, my intention is to bring the elements in their most raw form, not to regale you with the stories behind them. However, in the case of emotional sensitivity, I need to make an exception. The reason is simple: I can't come up with any other way to describe the importance of this element of the Psychological Safe Zone and how both elements work in conjunction with each other. And, most importantly, if I can describe how emotional sensitivity can be applied on the battlefield, then you will surely see it can be applied to the board room and, most importantly, to our personal lives as leaders.

The following story will not focus on the elements of the combat, but the principles of the leadership process. The background is as follows: in 2010, as an FBI Special Agent, I was attached to an Army Ranger Regiment in Afghanistan where we saw extensive combat operations. My primary responsibility was to collaborate with an Afghan interpreter, who had courageously volunteered to work with U.S. forces on these dangerous missions, to lead battlefield interviews after targets had been secured.

All operations were "kill or capture." I highlight this point to make clear that these were not run-of-the-mill operations (very few in war are). They were specifically targeted on individuals in leadership positions who had incentive to avoid being captured and, as such, surrounded themselves with loyal people who had incentive to avoid being captured or to prevent their leader from being captured. In short, we needed to do things correctly or the most severe consequences could be realized, all of which are unacceptable: mission failure, injury, or death.

Prior to each mission, the interpreter and I would discuss the target set to include the background of the target himself, any accomplices who may also be on target, the history of violence on the part of the target and accomplices, the presence of women and children on the target, and priorities depending on how much time we would have on target before we had to vacate, which could be anywhere from five minutes to one hour.

Just as how much time we would have on target varied, so too did the time we had for discussion prior to the operation, which could range, again, anywhere from only a few minutes to several hours.

Our strategies varied based on the priority of the target and very often around the cultural sensitivities at play. Or, more specifically, the presence of women and children on the target. We would discuss the circumstances under which it would be appropriate to physically move women from one area of the target to another, even though that meant simply holding the arm of the woman while escorting them. Or, if we decided we needed to interview a woman, how far away would we take them from their children? Would we take them out of view from everyone else on the target? Where and when would we search her person for weapons or explosives? What may be the consequences for that woman among her people after we leave the target because she was interviewed alone by Americans?

The interpreter would share what he felt were the cultural issues and potential consequences of deviating outside of cultural norms on the target, and we would both weigh these considerations against the importance of capturing, or otherwise locating, the actual target of the operation. While the final decision on our strategy was mine, we both expressed our opinions and ideas before every operation. All ideas were on the table and expressed freely, regardless of whether they were acted on. Our guideline: *Everyone feels like they can speak up and teammates speak in roughly the same proportion. Honest discussion can occur without fear of retribution or insult.*

About an hour into a patrol one night, en-route to our target location, our unit came under fire. We realized we were coming under friendly fire from a local Afghan Army unit. The patrol leader very quickly went about the business of sending all the standard non-verbal signals to relay to our Afghan partners that they were shooting at friendly forces. Unfortunately, to no avail. The patrol leader then called for the interpreter to come to his position. He was simply going to have the interpreter get on the mega-phone and tell the Afghans to stop shooting, as we were a friendly American force. No one in our patrol fired back at the Afghan unit.

There was no immediate movement toward the patrol leader. Given my role, I assumed it was my job to find the interpreter and bring him over to the patrol leader. Here is where I make my very important caveat:

By this point the incoming fire had become sporadic. I did not race through a hail of bullets to bring the interpreter to the patrol leader. People have done that and have been awarded appropriately for their bravery, selflessness, and heroism. That is not what I did. I did, however, have to run an adequate enough distance to find the interpreter and bring him back to the patrol leader. It was not heroism worthy, but it was also not the most comfortable thing I have ever done. And this is the point ...

When I got to the interpreter, I quickly tapped him on the back to get his attention and told him, "Let's go." As I turned to run back to the patrol leader, I quickly realized I was alone. I turned back to the interpreter and said again, "C'mon, let's go!"

His response left no room for interpretation, "No."

That interpreter had come under fire many times before. He was as brave and selfless as they come. He had never exhibited anything other than bravery and professionalism on operations. In that moment, however, he was just stuck. It doesn't matter why, and I never found out, or cared, why. But I had a decision to make.

I could have gone the macho, testosterone-fueled, impatient route and pulled him along while calling him names that questioned his manhood and courage. Or, I could exercise a little psychological safety, understand that he was stuck in the moment due to temporary fear or some other emotion, bend down and tell him, "It's ok. Trust me, it's ok." Which is what I did. He shook off whatever had him stuck and we continued with a successful mission ... right after he got on the megaphone and told the Afghans to stop shooting at us. Which they did.

I think this story breaks down the elements of the Psychological Safe Zone in a way that shows the research behind it is right on the mark and leaders at all levels should consider the Psychological Safe Zone as a guideline for behavior.

I've had leaders tell me they want to establish a culture of trust. The team needs to trust each other. As I outlined earlier, you can't just tell someone to trust you. They will not trust anyone just because they are directed that trust is now a part of the culture. The question we need to ask ourselves before we label an element of our desired culture, like trust, is, "What do we do to gain trust?"

The interpreter and I followed the guidelines for psychological safety to the letter. Each one of us was able to offer ideas to the other with the full knowledge that we would not be judged or laughed at. We both expressed our ideas fully and completely; neither one of us dominating the conversation. And at a moment of urgency, I recognized his emotional state of mind and acted appropriately by ensuring him everything was ok, to trust me.

And he did trust me. Not because I told him to, but because I had earned his trust (and he mine) by doing all the things the Psychological Safe Zone called for—consistently and all the time.

We established a culture by exercising psychological safety. What was the label we put on it? I have no idea because we never labeled it. For the sake of argument, let's call it a culture of trust. But we can call it trust only because of the things we did. Because of our behavior. Because of our Guidelines for Behavior. Not because we told each other that we needed to have trust, so we'd automatically trust each other. It simply does not work that way. What we DID established the trust.

You will also notice that the Psychological Safe Zone is not specific to combat. Yet, behaving in this way made us better warriors.

The point of discussing all the research on what makes great teams and of focusing on the Psychological Safe Zone is to establish a starting point for you, the leader, on Guidelines for Behavior. Another important thing to remember when it comes to Guidelines for Behavior is that no good behavior operates in a bubble. If you exercise a positive behavior it will have positive and impactful ripple effects into other areas of your life and organization. So too will negative behaviors.

CHAPTER NINE

Make Them Your Own— How to Define and Practice Guidelines for Behavior

GUIDELINES FOR BEHAVIOR ARE ESSENTIAL TO ANY GREAT leader, team, organization, or family. They establish what you will hold people accountable to. They move teams past the grind of industry best practices to a predictable behavioral environment that people love and will thrive in, regardless of profession or circumstance.

The work for establishing your Guidelines for Behavior comes from Elements One and Two of the leadership process: Emotional Awareness and Recognition and Cultural Awareness and Recognition. We cannot establish good behavioral guidelines if we are not first aware of what is actually happening to us and around us. Being aware of our emotions and the actions they drive, without judgement and for better or worse, will allow us to identify areas for improvement. It will allow us to establish what we will hold ourselves and the people we lead accountable to.

If you are struggling to define your behaviors, do your research. If you are reading this book you have probably read others like it that perhaps outline some leadership traits and behaviors that you like or are drawn towards. Try them out within the Guidelines for Behavior.

Remember, there are no absolutes. Guidelines for Behavior will be specific to you, the leader. They will reflect the needs of the organization and your personal behavioral compass.

Guidelines for Behavior are essential to the leadership process. However, choosing which Guidelines for Behavior are the right ones for you or your team requires some work. Welcome to the Art of Establishing Guidelines for Behavior. Some of your guidelines will remain forever because no matter how good you become at them they are the bedrock for how you do business. That's fine! As you fine-tune guidelines you may find that some can be retired because they were simple behaviors that have become ingrained and you are ready to move on to more advanced ones.

Unfortunately, sometimes your messages will get misinterpreted. Sometimes accidently, sometimes on-purpose. Either way, the messaging is your responsibility because you delivered it. You either delivered the message with clarity or with ambiguity. If you're not sure what I mean, ask yourself if your guideline for behavior can be interpreted any other way than how you meant it. Put yourself in the shoes of "that guy," the lowest common denominator who is always looking for a way around things. Keep this concept in the back of your mind as we move on to some other examples of Guidelines for Behavior. We'll come back to this.

To this day, one of the best leaders I ever encountered was my Commanding Officer at SEAL Team ONE. One of the many reasons was that he introduced me to the concept of Guidelines for Behavior. He laid out a series of short and very specific guidelines that he wanted his platoon leaders to abide by. If something went wrong, he could be counted on to bring you back to his guidelines for … guidance. They were behavioral guidelines that we were always accountable to.

Over the years, I used many of his guidelines for myself as a leader and began to incorporate my own as I got the hang of what Guidelines for Behavior were all about. What I ended up with was my own version of Guidelines for Behavior. At the time, these guidelines were primarily based on my experiences, both good and bad, as both a Surface Warfare Officer (ship driver) and Special Warfare Officer (SEAL). They also included experiences during my time in the private sector and at the United States Naval Academy. The following are the verbatim Guidelines for Behavior I presented to my first sales team in the private sector, circa 2000. As I look back on them, I'm forced to smile. Not because I don't believe in them, I do. I might have, however, used a slightly gentler touch, beginning with the name. Or maybe I wouldn't have …

Rules Set in Stone

I am a firm believer in guidelines and having a process in place to model how things should be done. I am also a firm believer that guidelines are just that; guidelines. They provide a road map that gives a general direction, not a course and speed that cannot be deviated from.

Having said that, I do have some rules that are set in stone and provide very little room for negotiation if violated.

1. **Be where you're supposed to be when you're supposed to be there.** If you are going to be late, call. If you don't know where you're supposed to be, call. If you make a call and tell me you are going to be late I will not ask you why. If it becomes a pattern, we will have a discussion and fix the problem.

2. **Pay attention to what is being discussed.** There is no greater inconsideration than having a sidebar conversation while someone else is talking. If you have something so important to say while someone else is speaking, politely interrupt and make your point. Being rude or appearing disinterested in what is being said is not something you would do with your customers, so I expect it will not be done with your teammates.

3. **Sell to the best of your ability.** I fully expect everyone to have an active life outside of (company name). However, during working hours, I expect all energy to be devoted to selling and making money. You will always be afforded the flexibility that comes with being

a salesperson. That's one of the reasons we get into this business. That flexibility does not extend to excessive smoke breaks, an abundance of personal calls, or general inactivity in the office. Those types of activities do not translate into selling to the best of your ability. If, from time to time, you have things to take care of and can only work half a day, fine. But work for half a day.

4. **Never lie or be deceitful.** I expect mistakes. I expect bad things to happen. I even expect some dumb things to happen. Just tell me the truth about these things so they can be fixed immediately and we can move on. My passion for this cannot be overstated. Of all the rules stated, the most dire consequences come with violating this one.

With the exception of these rules, no two people will be treated the same. No two people are the same, so common sense dictates that no two people should be treated the same. If I am kept abreast of developments in your account, if you are following the process and you are making sales, you can be confident I will stay out of your way. If you are not doing these things, well …

The Approach, Fallout, and Effect

Let's break these down first in the context of my approach. I let my boss review these before I sent them to my team. He approved. I was relocating from Washington, D.C. to New York City so I emailed my guidelines (or, "Rules Set in Stone"), to my new team for review prior to meeting them for the first time. My intention was to set the expectations early and give everyone a chance to digest them. I wasn't blind to how these guidelines would come across to my new team as such clarity and straightforwardness is usually reserved for military discussion.

About a day after I sent them to the team, I got a call from my boss. He advised me that the team was not happy, and I could expect mutiny when I arrived. I was a little surprised. Not so much at the team's reaction (although "mutiny" seemed a little strong), but at my boss' delivery of the message. "I ran these by you before I sent them out. You said you were good with them," I said.

He responded, "I am. I love them. I just wanted to give you a heads-up as to what you are walking into. Good luck," he concluded with the subtlety of a sledgehammer.

I appreciated the heads-up and put together my plan for the initial meeting with my team. I believed in and trusted what I was doing so I had no concern about addressing the issue head-on and immediately. So I began, "Hello, my name is Errol. I'm happy to be your new manager. I understand there are some concerns with the document I sent everyone to review. Please address your concerns freely."

"Freely" was barely out of my mouth when the onslaught began.

"We're not your soldiers in the military!"

"How dare you treat us like children!"

"Are you calling us liars?"

"I've got ten years more sales experience than you have. What do you even know?"

I'm pretty sure there was a reference to Hitler in there as well.

After the initial salvo was complete I asked, "Is that it?" I absorbed one or two more glancing blows, and then continued, "OK, I've heard everything you've said, and I understand how you feel. I'll make you a deal. Let's go over each one of these rules, and if you can make an argument as to why any of these behaviors should not be required, we will take them off. And, you don't even have to make a good argument. Just an argument."

Was my approach the right approach? I have no idea. If I had to do it today, I would probably make some adjustments to delivery and wording. Specifically, with the word "rules." But what I believed in was the message, so I had no problem with defending the rules to a hostile crowd. I believed, based on my experience and personal beliefs, that even if we didn't change the explicit ways we made, marketed, or sold our widget, but changed our behaviors to align with my rules, we would get better as a sales team.

How does the story end? Happily! Of course, nobody could deny that it was better to be on time than late, for example. They just didn't like being told that. When I explained why these things were so important to me, and what I saw when these things weren't done, the sales team started to understand and get on board. Furthermore, when I asked if anyone had never seen these behaviors, or that if things like gossiping made teams better, once again, everyone understood where I was coming from; I simply wanted to be clear about the behaviors I would be holding them accountable to. By the end of the meeting, everyone was very comfortable with where we stood, and we went on to have a hugely successful team. Nothing was taken off the list.

Your approach to successfully delivering Guidelines for Behavior will come with experience. Unfortunately, there is no way around that fact. But how to deliver the message, and the message itself, are two different topics. We are focused on the message of Guidelines for Behavior. If you believe in the concept of Guidelines for Behavior and you give thought to which Guidelines for Behavior are important to you, the leader, then your message will get through.

Another important element to good Guidelines for Behavior is that they are unambiguous. Guidelines for Behavior should be put in some context, even something as simple as "be on time." Ensure you clear up what "be on time" means to you. If you say, "we start at 9:00 a.m." and someone dives through the door at exactly 9:00 a.m., are they on time? Or perhaps 9:00 a.m. means "we will actually start the meeting at 9:00 a.m., so please be in your seats ready to go." These are small differences, but differences that need to be cleared up. However, the general guideline is clear and unambiguous. Nobody can turn it on its head to their benefit. For example, nobody can say, "Be on time? Oh, I thought you actually meant to be late." Remember "that guy" I referenced earlier? The one who will turn anything you say on its head to his (or her) benefit?

Make your guidelines clear and unambiguous, with necessary clarity and context provided, and you will have effectively and professionally neutralized your lowest common denominator.

Making Guidelines that Stick

Let's talk briefly about how to make your guidelines stick so you can make the simple reprimand everyone will understand, "That's not how we do business around here."

One thing that happens a lot is that leaders put out what they want from their teams once. Maybe they put it out in a document, and maybe they even have people sign the document. "We pledge to …" and then nobody sees the document again, maybe ever. The leader might have actually identified Guidelines for Behavior in the document, but does this scenario meet with the spirit of what is trying to be achieved? Of course not. So, what to do?

If something is important enough to be said once, it is important enough to say over and over … and over again. If you believe in Guidelines for Behavior and go about the business of identifying them, telling everyone one time what they are will not cut it. "Ok, Errol, how often should we review them with our teams?"

The answer is simple, a lot!

However often it takes so you can eventually get to the one sentence reprimand everyone will understand, "That's not how we do business around here."

Once a week? Yes. Once a month? Yes. Once a quarter? Yes. Every time a guideline is violated? Yes. Often enough so the Guideline for Behavior becomes part of your culture; the thing you do.

Best Practices vs. Guidelines for Behavior

The New York FBI SWAT Team was as good a combat team I've ever been associated with. While SWAT was a collateral duty in the FBI, we trained regularly, and we trained hard. The overwhelming majority of our work was close quarters battle (CQB). Essentially, CQB is the process of going into a house to arrest or locate a subject (bad guy). We were constantly honing and identifying CQB best practices, which are not to be mistaken for Guidelines for Behavior.

Best practices included things like how to enter a room properly and efficiently, how to clear a hallway, how to navigate a hallway intersection, how to throw a flashbang into a room when the door is closed and when the door is open. Best practices seem to always change or be modified, which is good. This means you are always thinking about how to do your job better. On SWAT, we would drill the best practices until we had them down. Remember: *If you didn't change the way you make, market, or sell your widget, but behave in these ways, you will get better.*

Therefore, best practices don't fall under Guidelines for Behavior because they are specific to your widget. In this case, CQB. Our Guidelines for Behavior while conducting CQB were the constant. No matter what happened, if things were going badly or we forgot how to execute a new best practice, we could always go back to our guidelines to get through a situation successfully. We had three guidelines on the New York SWAT Team:

- Read off the operator in front of you.
- Cover your buddy.
- Find work.

How often did we review these guidelines? Every time we practiced CQB. On a single day of training CQB we might have gone through 50 to 100 practice runs. How often did we review the Guidelines for Behavior? 50 to 100 times a day. Every critique of a best practice would inevitably fall under a Guideline for Behavior.

For example, let's say the best practice was for the first operator to enter a room and go to the left, the next operator to go right, and the third operator to go to the center. Now, let's say the first operator goes to the left, but the second operator goes to the center instead of the right. You, as the third operator, know that you are supposed to go to the center. So, what do you do? Well, the best practice says for you to go to the center, but if you go to the center, as per the best practice, you will leave the right side of the room uncovered and potentially put all your fellow operators at risk (because maybe the bad guy is hiding in the corner of the right side of the room with a gun!). You will be technically correct if you go to the center, but it is not the correct decision.

Remember, Guidelines for Behavior bring us back on track when things are going wrong. In this instance, things went wrong as soon as the second operator went to the center of the room instead of the right side of the room. So, as the third operator, you go back to your Guidelines for Behavior that have been drilled in your brain in what seems like an endless fashion. But now you realize why. Because you, as the third operator, immediately go to them for answers. In this case, you can pick one of two behaviors that will fix the situation.

Read off the operator in front of you. The number two operator went to the center instead of the right. Therefore, I will read off their movement and go to the right. The number three operator has just avoided a potential life-threatening situation by following a simple guideline for behavior. Common sense? Yes. Common practice? No! Simply stated, I've seen countless number three operators go to the center even though the number two operator was already there.

Cover your buddy. This behavior will net the same result, but with a different thought process. Using the same scenario, the number three operator simply identifies that the right side of the room is not covered by anyone. Further, the number three operator knows that there could potentially be a threat on the right side of the room that could have devastating results on their teammates. (Remember the bad guy!) So, the number three operator goes to the right to cover his buddy.

For the sake of thoroughness, let's look at another example for the last guideline, find work. When conducting CQB, operators generally form a single line as they move through the house. The operators who get caught toward the end of the line don't always get much action, i.e.: room entries. That's ok, it's just the way it goes sometimes. What happens sometimes is that the operators at the end of the line may tend to lose a little focus. The third guideline will ensure that this does not happen.

If the operators toward the end of the line are trying to find work, guess what they are not doing? Staring at the head of the operator in front of them waiting for their turn to enter a room and potentially losing focus. Instead, they notice a chair or table that may inhibit movement toward the next room. So, they jump out of the line, move the obstacle, and get back in line. Or, they notice one of the operators in the front of the line may need a flashbang to enter a room and they don't appear to have one. So, they jump out of line, give the operator their flashbang, and get back in line.

The point is, there is usually something you can be doing. If you have not actually found work, then you are always actively looking. This keeps you focused and, more importantly, assists the overall efficiency of the operation. Find work is not specific to CQB, but it makes the SWAT team better at CQB. Therefore, it is a great example of a Guideline for Behavior.

How It Works at Home

My premise has been that The Process, Art, and Science of Leadership is applicable to every aspect of life: combat, business, and your personal life at home. We've covered business and combat so let's talk about the home.

New Years is a time of great hope and new beginnings. Every year we try to make positive adjustments to our life. We put forward a list of very specific goals, and actions we are going to take to achieve those goals. This is all good! I'm not about to suggest that new beginnings, goals, and actions aren't positive. What I am going to suggest, however, is that perhaps we generally go about it all wrong. I think we tend to focus too much on the specific actions, or best practices if you will, when we should focus instead on Guidelines for Behavior.

My family is no different. This past New Year's my wife and I sat down to look for common areas of growth together. We immediately focused on the master bedroom and bathroom. As we were embarrassed to admit, we were trending backwards and occasionally resembled teenagers in the way we straightened up and cleaned our bedroom and bathroom. Three small children, three dogs, and two working parents will do that to you if you let it. Guests were not going to stroll into our bedroom, so best to focus cleaning on the kitchen, family room, living room, and anywhere else a guest may roam into. But enough was enough and it was time to act like adults and set the right example for our children. Our bedroom and bathroom would be the cleanest parts of the house! (Did I mention how embarrassing this is?)

So, we resolved to deep clean the bedroom and bathroom once a week. We made a list of what would be cleaned when and who was responsible. All good, right? We set a specific goal and identified actions.

But something felt wrong with the process. Yes, we needed to be tidier, but was this really something that was going to make us better all around? Wasn't there a behavior that would cover tidying up the master bedroom, but also benefit other areas of our life? Is this really what our life's goals had come down to? "Clean the toilet" as a New Year's resolution?

Read off the operator in front of you, cover your buddy, find work. YES! These were behaviors we could apply, or resolve to, that would make us better without focusing on just cleaning the toilet! We ended up combining all three into one behavior, but all three were in play. So, what does this look like?

If my wife is cleaning the dishes, I grab the garbage. If my wife is dressing our son for school, I make sure our daughter is eating her breakfast. If I am getting frustrated helping our son with his homework, my wife steps in and gives me a break so he gets the attention and positive energy he needs.

What else? Find work. I have a couple of minutes to spare and pass by that stack of mail on the counter. (Yes, you know that stack of mail!) I grab a handful and clear it out. I'm brushing my teeth and notice the counter is getting a little crusty. I grab a Clorox wipe and wipe it down while I'm brushing my teeth. Dishes are stacking up, but I don't have time to do them all. But, I have time to do a few, so I do a few. I've found 15 minutes! Instead of turning on a mindless television show or randomly surfing the web, I remember we have three dogs and go clean as much of the yard as I can.

You get it. When we focus on the behavior a lot of different things get done that very soon make life easier and more orderly.

How about this for finding work? My daughter has had a rough day and isn't her normal happy-go-lucky self. So, my wife puts down everything she is doing and sits with her for a little while to comfort her and show her the love she clearly needs. How do we recognize found work? We go back to Chapter 7 and remember that, as leaders, we are always in the moment and aware of what is happening to us and around us. Because we are in the moment and aware, we can identify what either needs to be done or can be done. Because we are in the moment, we can step outside ourselves and find work.

CHAPTER TEN

Implementing Your Guidelines for Behavior

I LOVED BEING A SPECIAL AGENT FOR THE FBI. SOME OF THE greatest leaders I have ever met sat in the FBI offices in New York City and led amazing cases that had profound impact in New York City, the United States, and around the world. However in my opinion, those great leaders in the FBI I am speaking of were outliers, not the norm.

When we speak of leadership, the main difference between my experience in the SEAL Teams and the FBI was that good leaders, and the expectancy of good leadership, was the norm in the SEAL Teams and poor leaders were the outliers.

In my opinion, the FBI was the opposite. Poor leaders and the expectancy of poor leadership was the norm and good leaders were the outliers.

I bring this up not to take a gratuitous shot at the FBI. I bring it up to highlight that, despite loving the job of FBI Special Agent, the environment drove me away. As I spent time in New York City I would see consistent flashes of poor leadership that I had a hard time believing were really happening. Half-truths, lies, jealousy, vindictiveness, "my way or the highway," laziness, outsized and misplaced ego, gossip and pettiness. It was hard to believe. But it wasn't until I left the New York Office and transferred to a much smaller office in a different state did I fully realize the overall corrosive environment I was a part of.

Every single Guideline for Behavior I cite in this section was not only lacking in that smaller office, the culture consisted of the opposite behaviors. Lateness to meetings and not paying attention or otherwise rude behavior during meetings were the norm. Half-truths and innuendo were treated as fact. In some cases, so was straight lying. When an idea was put on the table for discussion, you could count on gossip, bad-mouthing, and mean spiritedness to follow. A few people forcefully and rudely dominated conversation.

Here's the really disturbing thing: that behavior was prevalent in only a small handful of people. Yet, it prevailed and poisoned the overall culture and morale of the office. Why and how? I watched "leader" after "leader" come through that office and tolerate the anti-social and unprofessional behavior of a few. Because the "leaders" tolerated, and in many instances took part in, the behavior I described, it became the fabric and reputation of the office.

It didn't matter that the vast majority of the people in the office were good people. They were forced to accept the wholly objectionable behavior of a few because it was tolerated and often promulgated by "leadership."

What's my point here? It is to reiterate that leaders set the tone for behavior. A few people of bad intention and character can poison an entire team if left unchecked by one person; the leader. The team can fight these people and marginalize them, but only if their resolve to fight is matched by the leader. Otherwise, negativity will prevail.

I loved being a Navy SEAL because of both the job and the environment created by the great people and leaders of the SEAL Team community. I loved being a copier salesman because of the safe and predictable environment that was created by the leader—not because I loved selling copiers. I loved doing the work of an FBI Special Agent. But the environment and the prevalent behaviors inside the FBI put me in the position to decide; stay or leave? So, I left.

My position is that leaders should focus on creating an environment people love, and that an environment people love is one that is predictable. Remember one of the examples I gave previously: If the leader treats you one way today and another way tomorrow ... that's an unpredictable environment people will grow tired of. If teammates can vent, criticize, and demean at the whim of their emotions without having to answer to the leader for their behavior ... that's an unpredictable environment people will grow tired of.

Where To Start

I understand that if you are reading this book you may be in the middle of a difficult situation like I described at the FBI. So, what to do? How and where do you start the process of turning things around? Well, the only good place to start anything is the place you actually start. Don't wait for the perfect opportunity or for things to slow down. There is no perfect opportunity and things won't slow down. Understand this as a fact and it will be easier to start. There is no wrong time to begin positive change.

That said, how you implement what you believe is, again, different from what you believe. You must first work to understand the principle behind Guidelines for Behavior.

If we didn't change the way we made, marketed, or sold our widget, but behaved in these ways, would we get better?

Identify one or two behaviors and ask yourself at the end of each day if you did them. Steal a couple from my examples and take them for a test drive. Ask yourself at the end of each day if you "found work" or "finished what you started." Be conscious, or in the moment, as to their impact on your personal and professional life. Then try some others. Be on time, listen, don't gossip or bad-mouth, etc., and do the same thing; be conscious of their impact on your personal and professional life.

The next challenge is to implement them in your team. I'm not hiding or running away from the fact that this will be difficult. It will. Welcome to leadership! I can't tell you how to do it because I'm not you. How I do it may not work for you because we are two different people. You will have to experiment. You will have to see what works for you and what doesn't. You will have to summon the courage to fail, adjust, fail a little less, adjust, and continue to rinse and repeat until you have found your formula. I can, however, offer a couple of suggestions to get you started.

How To Get Your Team Started

Begin with one guideline—a simple one that everyone gets and that you can easily begin doing. "Be on time" or "pay attention" are easy ones that will begin the process. Nobody will look at you sideways if you begin saying that you expect everyone to be on time and pay attention. Why? Because everyone will agree with you! Now, just because they agree with you does not mean they will obey you. Strange, but true. We'll cover this in "The Resistance."

You may or may not give explanation to your new guidelines. Again, experience will give you this answer. But, begin mentioning the behavior out loud and you are making it clear that people are now answerable, or accountable, to that behavior. Besides getting people to be on time and paying attention, you are doing something else; you are beginning the process of setting Guidelines for Behavior. So, when you throw in another one, it will be less of a splash of cold water in everyone's face. You will have begun the process of making the behavioral environment predictable. You will have begun establishing what people are going to be held accountable to.

Perhaps you could go a little more formal. Perhaps you

could begin with one or two of the simple behaviors and sit everyone down and explain what is on your mind and why you are even bringing this up. Maybe it looks something like this:

> I want to address something that has been bothering me for some time. I'm sure I'm not the only one who notices that our meetings never really begin on time. First, let me say it's my fault. For such a small behavior, I believe it has a negative impact on our overall performance and culture. When we are not on time, I believe it sends a message to everyone that we are not respectful of each other's time. And if we are not respectful of each other's time, it begs the question of what else we are not respectful of regarding each other. I believe it chips away at fundamental trust. That said, I'd like all of us to be conscious of being on time. For me, that means if the meeting is scheduled to start at 9:00 a.m., everyone is seated and ready to begin at 9:00 a.m. For my part, I will not only abide by this, but will also address lateness until being on time becomes a habit for our team. It's a small thing, but if we do it right and consistently, I believe it will have a positive impact.

Substitute "pay attention," "no gossip or bad-mouthing," or "no lies or half-truths" for "be on time" for the guideline of your choice. Or, imagine gradually incorporating each one after "be on time" has become a habit. This is an easy and effective way to begin, especially if you are in the middle of a bad situation. Take it one step at a time.

Perhaps these very basic behavioral guidelines don't apply to your team. Maybe you see room for improvement, but these basic behaviors are already in place. Fantastic! Then you can jump in with things like, "find work" or "we finish what we start" or "we look for answers before we ask questions." Navy SEAL ethos dictates things like "prioritize and execute," "decentralize command," and the need to keep things simple. These are excellent Guidelines for Behavior if you already have a team that is operating at a high level but still has room for growth.

Implementing Guidelines for Behavior toes a fine line between being aggressive and being patient. You see that they are important, and you are anxious to begin implementing them. Good! However, you also know that hitting everyone over the head with them may not be the best approach. So, don't. Be aggressive but be patient. Be consistent, but not overbearing.

Consistency and clarity will get you there. You may be worried that you'll come across as inauthentic or hypocritical because you're always late. Nothing is more authentic than honestly admitting a fault and deciding you are going to work to improve it.

So, when you hear, "What's up, Errol? Suddenly you are telling us how to act and what to do? You're never on time! A bit hypocritical, don't you think?"

Your response to this is simple, because it's true, "I know. And it's a bad behavior that has a negative impact on everyone. That is why I'm going to change it in myself and ask the same of the team. I want to get better. I want our team to get better.

I can't change how I acted in the past, but I can change this behavior going forward."

What's important is that you believe in the message and you do your best to deliver it positively in a way that fits your personality. Again, it will be difficult if you are in the middle of a tough situation. Trust in this process, though. It will begin to create the environment people love to be a part of.

Too Many Is None

There is no need to pile on Guidelines for Behavior. One to three behaviors will do the trick because good behavior does not operate in a bubble, it will have positive effects outside the behavior itself. Imagine if you and/or your team performed the following behaviors flawlessly: prioritize and execute to completion, plan before we act, operate in a Psychological Safe Zone. (Remember the research?) If you did these three things well, would you get better? Would you get significantly better? Yes, you would. One to three is plenty!

So, let's break down the leadership process to this point. Emotions drive our actions. We must be situationally aware of our emotions in order to drive the actions we want. Culture is made up of the things you do, not the labels you put on them. Just like our emotions, we must be situationally aware of the things we and those around us do to identify our current culture. Once you identify what you and those around you do that make up your current culture, you are in a position to define what you want to do, or how you want to behave, by identifying Guidelines for Behavior.

Now you, the leader, are establishing what you and your team do that makes up your culture as well as what you will hold people accountable to.

Practicing the Art

Once you've established what you want for your Guidelines for Behavior, the real challenge will come with implementing them. No matter how you decide to implement them, doing so will take one overwhelming characteristic: courage.

Before we step into an ice bath, we do certain things to prepare. We breathe to obtain a mental and emotional focus as well as dulling our pain receptors. When we are in the ice bath, we are in the moment and focused on our breath to remain calm amidst the chaos the ice bath represents. When we exit the ice bath, we maintain focus and begin the process of warming ourselves in a controlled fashion by way of an exercise called the horse stance. There is only one place where process is not a part of the equation; when we decide to step into the ice bath.

As much as you prepare to get in, you still must decide. You still must summon the courage to do something your every instinct is telling you not to, even though you know the benefits will be massive and long-lasting. You will either act with courage and get in, or act with cowardice and not get in.

Now, relax. I'm not challenging your ego here with the word "cowardice," and I'm not calling you a coward. However, the simple fact remains if you make the decision to get in the ice bath, it is a courageous one. If you make the decision not to get in, it is the opposite of courage … cowardice.

By consistently stepping into the ice bath, day after day, week after week, and year after year, you are conditioning your brain to make courageous decisions. You are building a habit. You are creating a Guideline for Behavior that will pave the way to implement your personal or team Guidelines for Behavior: "I act with courage." Does it meet the test? If you act with courage in your decision-making process, will you get better? I think yes.

If you act with courage, and implement your Guidelines for Behavior at work, at home, or in your personal life, will you get better? Yes!

You must practice anything to be good at it. Courage is no different. Stepping into an ice bath will help you practice making courageous decisions because implementing your Guidelines for Behavior will take courage.

Courage is just one example of a behavioral guideline you can practice by practicing cold exposure. Think about the cold exposure drill you did during Cultural Awareness and Recognition. What did you observe about yourself before stepping into an ice bath or cold shower? Did you procrastinate? Did you make excuses to not get in? Did you not turn the shower to all the way cold? Did you hoot and holler when you got in and over-dramatize the entire experience?

Choose a Behavior and Provide Context

Now decide how you want to behave in the cold. You may decide you want to act like a professional. Acting like a professional may mean something a little different to all of us so it is important to identify what it means to you. Perhaps to you it means not overreacting to an external stimulus, like the cold ... or that co-worker. Now you have a clear idea what the behavior looks like and can go about working on it.

You now know what the effect of focusing on one thing has on your brain and what focusing on your breath and ensuring a conscious exhale has on your nervous system. It calms you down. So, with that in mind you enter the ice bath, you recognize the fight or flight effects of the cold and focus on your breath. When all the external factors that the cold will drive you towards come to the surface (Get me out of here! It's too cold! How much longer? I hate this! I can't do this anymore!), you acknowledge them and move your focus back to your breath. No matter how many times your mind wanders, you bring it back to your breath.

Soon enough, you will be entering and remaining in the cold like a professional. No overly-dramatic displays of emotion. No excuses or focus on external environmental factors. Just focus and calm, like a professional.

Context is vital to behavioral guidelines and will allow you focus and act with intention. Maybe defining the behavior as acting like a professional doesn't work for you. However, you like the idea of recognizing your emotions and focusing on your breath as behaviors. That's fine, these are still behaviors and they mean more to you than the idea of acting like a professional, so go with those.

This is why cold exposure is vital to practicing the Art of Guidelines for Behavior. It will allow you to define exactly the behavior you want to work on as an individual. When you are able to provide that focus for your own personal behaviors, you will be in a much better position to identify them for your team. You will be able to display empathy and understanding for what needs change. Then, you will be able to put into context the necessary behaviors to create the culture you want for your team by identifying what behaviors you will be holding your team accountable to.

When Everything Stays the Same, Nothing Changes

Back in the 1900's scientists conducted a study on rodents to see if new neurons could grow in the brain. The scientists concluded it was not possible. It appeared we were doomed to our current state of brain function.[69]

Later, however, the study of neurogenesis told us this was inaccurate. In fact, the brain can grow new neurons. When you learn new things and have new experiences you make new connections and grow new neurons.[70][71] It's called neuroplasticity; the brain's ability to reorganize itself by forming new neural connections throughout life. Neuroplasticity allows neurons to adjust their activities in response to new situations or changes in the environment. In other words, the brain can rewire itself and grow new neurons when it's stimulated by new things or experiences.[72][73]

So, what was wrong with the rodent study where scientists concluded that the brain could not produce new neurons? The rodent's environment never changed. So, because their environment never changed, they had no new thoughts or experiences, so their brains stayed the same.[74]

Remember what the research said about us? We have between 60,000-70,000 thoughts in one day and 80 to 90% of those thoughts are the same as the day before.[75] For most people, 70% of the time those thoughts are associated with the hormones and emotions of stress: anger, jealousy, frustration, worthlessness, fear, anxiety, insecurity, guilt, envy, etc.[76] Now we know that when everything stays the same, nothing changes. And we further know that very little of what we do or think changes. And we wonder why we can't make positive change in our lives when we think and do the same things over and over!

If You Change Things, Things Will Change

TRIGGER to EMOTION to THINK/DECIDE to ACT. Your new behavioral guidelines are the first things you should think about inside of "THINK/DECIDE." You have done the hard work of observing your current culture, or what you do. In exercising the Art of Guidelines for Behavior you identified what you want to do or how you want to behave. You have exercised courage in your decision making, perhaps. When you did that you experienced something new and created a new emotion. And, the results were likely good because we moved away from those emotions and actions of stress.

Or, perhaps you behaved with patience, empathy, gratitude, grace, or love as part of your new behaviors. Maybe you focused on finding your breath during stressful times. Maybe you prioritized and executed to completion. Maybe you found work or covered your buddy or planned before you acted. Regardless, you moved to conscious action that is positive.

When you did this the neurons in your brain began to form new networks and the brain began to make new chemicals to replace the ragged, tired, and destructive chemicals produced by your previous negative behaviors and emotions of stress. Then you did it over and over and the new neuropathways in your brain became stronger and stronger as the old ones faded away because they were not being used anymore.

And now you are acting with courage or grace or love or gratitude or focus. The more you act with it, the more you become it and eventually it becomes your personality. It has become what you do because you have literally changed your mindset by simply identifying a positive behavior that produces new experiences and new emotions. You are no longer the rat in an unchanging environment who never changes and wonders why.

I'm not sure I can paint with any broader brush when it comes to this portion of the science. But it should give you what you need to appreciate and understand the impact the Process, Art, and Science of Leadership will have on your life from a scientific standpoint. In short, to make changes you must come out of your current, perhaps stagnant, state and make a decision about your current behavior and what you want to replace it with. You have to feel the impact of that decision because it must create an emotional experience greater than the one you are replacing it with.

CHAPTER ELEVEN

Element Four—The Planning Process

W HEN WE MEET WITH FAILURE IN OUR LIVES, WE BECOME very adept at assigning blame to outside forces. There wasn't enough time, people weren't committed, we didn't have the resources, Alien invasion, or it just wasn't meant to be.

Here's the hard truth: Failure comes from one reason and one reason only ... bad planning. We fail because we don't cover the consistent and proven elements necessary to achieve success. The ones that give us the right questions to ask. The ones that allow our people to work with initiative and autonomy. The ones that allow us to unemotionally prioritize and then methodically execute.

Each element of the leadership process builds on the one before it. We started with Emotional Awareness and Recognition because emotions drive our Actions. Then we moved to Cultural Awareness and Recognition because culture is the sum total of the Actions we take; those Actions ultimately make up our culture. And then we identified what Actions we want to make up our culture, so we established Guidelines for Behavior that would begin the process of identifying what we would hold people accountable to.

The first three elements of the process allow the leader to create a predictable environment people will love to be a part of. But ultimately, leaders need to drive Mission accomplishment. And to drive Mission accomplishment, leaders need to plan with precision and discipline.

The Planning Process will be broken down into three chapters. This chapter will break down each element of the Planning Process in detail as a project management tool. The next chapters will go over how the Planning Process is used as a leadership tool and will cover things like how it helps prioritization, creates initiative, and allows you to work under pressure in a calm and methodical fashion.

Modified Navy SEAL Planning

Let's begin with the breakdown of the Planning Process. This process is a simplified and modified version of the process I learned and used as Navy SEAL Platoon Commander. The reason I bring this up is because it serves as a reminder that the operations we conducted in the SEAL Teams tended to be dangerous and if we didn't consciously account for each element of the Planning Process we ran the risk of missing one. And if we missed one of the elements, the chances of something going wrong increased exponentially. And the something "going wrong" could mean one of three things: Mission failure, injury, or death. All three of which are completely unacceptable, especially if they could be reasonably avoided by simply following the elements of the Planning Process.

The beauty of this process is that its effectiveness on the battlefield is 100% transferable to the boardroom and the kitchen table. It can be used for massive initiatives, the small fires that seem to plague us by the hour, or the internal struggles we face daily, both at work and at home.

The elements of the Planning Process form the acronym SMACCC, which stands for Situation, Mission, Actions, Contingencies, Command, and Communication. Now, let's go over each element and how to apply it.

SMACCC: "Situation"

The Situation is the set of background circumstances dictating a need for Action.

Why are you doing something or why are you about to do something? To make it clearer, if you hear someone describe a scenario and your response is, "Well what are we doing about that?" or "We need to do something about that," then the Situation has been clearly identified because it specifically lays out the need for Action.

If your response is, "So What?" then you don't have a need for Action. You've just saved yourself and your team a lot of wasted time by clearly determining if a set of circumstances dictates a need for Action. The Situation is not always geared toward a problem. A set of circumstances dictating a need for Action can be an opportunity as well. The crux of the Situation is that if you fail to act on the given set of circumstances that require Action, it will have a negative impact on your work or life.

The Situation instills the overall sense of purpose. As the work trickles down to the line level workers, they should always understand why they are doing something ... or be able to ask the leader why they are doing something and get a clear and concise answer.

The Situation must be defined by the leader. If the leader does not define the Situation, then work is getting done randomly and without purpose. Projects will die a quick death or take sharp drastic turns that seem to have no rhyme or reason simply because people don't know why they are doing what they are doing.

Teams often act on circumstances that they don't really need to act on, or at least not right then, because they have not first evaluated whether a set of circumstances will negatively impact their work if left unchecked. That evaluation helps determine the Actions that are necessary. Making sure you understand the circumstances and the potential negative impacts of Action and inaction will ensure you and your team are acting on things that really matter and will impact your organization, team, or family.

Think about those fires that plague you every day. If you've ever bothered to ask what the Situation was, or why you were asked to do that particular thing IMMEDIATELY, did you get a clear and concise answer that would allow you to properly prioritize that work because you understood the importance of it?

If you have asked for the Situation, how often was the answer akin to something like, "Well, Jan said it needed to be done," and it was left at that. So often we either don't ask the Situation, don't tell somebody the Situation, or nobody knows the Situation. Hence, we're not even sure why we are doing the work we are doing. But we do it. And then we have a million fires to contend with before we know it.

The Situation is the element of the Planning Process most frequently overlooked or under-communicated. Perhaps because it takes a little extra effort to articulate why we want people to go in a particular direction. Yes, it does take more work up-front to clearly identify and articulate the background circumstances that have led to the need for Action. But without the clarification, focus, efficiency, and purpose are lost … and results or Mission success suffer.

When you ask someone, "Why?" you are really just asking them to articulate the Situation. (Might this be a Guideline for Behavior to consider? Ask "Why?")

SMACCC: "Mission"

A Mission is simply your goal; what you are specifically trying to achieve.

You have identified your Situation, or set of circumstances that determine a need for Action. If you have determined you need to act, then you need to act with a specific purpose. Or, you need to have a clearly defined Mission. Your Mission is what you're going to do about the Situation.

Whatever you want to accomplish needs to be clearly defined—everyone on your team needs to know exactly what the Mission is, and exactly what you're trying to accomplish. Having a clearly-defined Mission sounds like common sense, and it is. But it's not always common practice. Disagreements on issues that seem to take a million different directions are often mitigated quickly when we can remind each other what we are specifically trying to accomplish, or what the Mission is.

If you are confused as to whether you or one of your people should do a certain thing or perform a certain task, all you have to do is ask yourself if that task gets you closer to accomplishing your Mission. If the task does get you closer to your Mission, then you have your answer. It's generally that simple. But, like the Situation, the Mission is not always clearly defined or articulated by the leader. Sometimes the Mission is unclear because several Missions have been identified as one big Mission. You may very well find you have several Missions that need to be accomplished. That's fine; simply break them out individually so they are clear.

The leader identifies the Situation and sets the Mission.

SMACCC: "Actions"

Actions are the steps that need to be accomplished to complete the Mission.

Along with identifying what Actions need to take place to accomplish the Mission, we also need to identify when those

Actions will be completed. It doesn't matter how complex or simple the Actions are ... if they are not identified then they either won't get done or you are hoping or assuming they will get done. Remember what we say about hope and assumptions: they have no place in the leadership process.

Identify the Actions that need to take place to accomplish the Mission. Identify when those Actions are to be completed.

Who should identify the Actions? We'll cover that in the Art of SMACCC. For now, as a leader just know that Actions and when they will be completed need to be identified for an effective plan to take place.

SMACCC: "Command"

Command designates specific people to be responsible and accountable for completing specific Actions for the Mission.

If an Action needs to take place then there needs to be a name next to it to clearly identify who is in charge of, or in Command of, that Action.

Once we clearly identify the Actions that need to take place to accomplish our Mission, Command needs to be assigned to those Actions. Once again, if we are not assigning Command next to an Action, then we are either hoping or assuming it will get done. Leaders don't hope and assume. They make clear who is in Command of getting each Action accomplished.

The same is true for the overall Mission. One person is in Command of the Mission. One person must be given authority to make decisions inside the clearly defined Mission. One person. Leadership by committee is no leadership at all.

Command is not, "I command you to do this!" Command is the act of assigning who is in charge of what.

This is where the company's organizational chart, or dotted lines of authority, get thrown out the window. Why? Because each Mission should have its own organizational chart. So, in the overall hierarchy of your organization, you and another person may be peers, so you've got no authority over them in the overall scheme and context of your organization. That's fine.

However, for a particular project, or Mission, when one person assumes Command then they have overall authority over that Mission regardless of what the company organizational chart says. This is why we need clearly defined Command for every Mission and every Action—it establishes final decision-making authority. Final decision-making authority inside a Mission is critical because, again, leadership by committee is no leadership at all.

Remember, we can't hold people accountable if they don't know what they are supposed to be accountable to. Inside the Planning Process, assigning Command makes it clear what people will be held accountable to, whether it's the overall Mission or each Action inside the Mission.

SMACCC: "Contingencies"

We must plan for the things that can go wrong by identifying Contingencies for each Action.

Contingencies are defined as "something that might possibly happen in the future, usually causing problems or making further arrangements necessary." When we identify Actions, we obviously feel like those Actions are the appropriate ones required to achieve our Mission. The reality, however, tells us that sometimes things go wrong. A good plan accounts for the things that can go wrong by identifying Contingency plans for each Action.

Look at each Action and identify a couple of things that can go wrong and then account for them. This concept is simple but can get tricky. How much time should we spend on how we will execute each Contingency? Does each Contingency require an entire new plan? I can think of 100 things that can go wrong; we can't account for each one!

Planning for Contingencies will be the hardest thing you do. You will find there are either a million potential problems that come to mind, or none at all. It takes practice and experience to get these right, so don't worry about perfection when you're just getting started. Start by at least thinking about them and the Contingencies will find you. We will discuss some of the nuances inside of Contingencies in the next chapter. For now, it is important that you should know to account for Contingencies. As long as you are constantly asking yourself, "What can go wrong with this Action?" you will quickly build your experience base and become increasingly adept at understanding the depth and detail you need to put into the Contingencies. Some Contingencies will be running Contingencies, meaning you will always be accounting for them. Some will be very specific. Experience will be your guide. But to gain the necessary experience, you must always begin the process of accounting for Contingencies.

Let me share a couple of simple examples from both combat and business. My combat example is hardly exciting, but it highlights the importance of Contingency planning even in the simplest of scenarios.

When I was a Platoon Commander in the SEAL Teams, I had just briefed an operation to my Commanding Officer. He approved the operation, which included when rehearsals were to be conducted before we left for the operation. Later in the day I checked in with him to give him an update and he asked me if rehearsals had been conducted. I replied that we had conducted rehearsals for the Actions on target.

Then he asked if we had rehearsed loading the helicopter. I was a bit confused, so I asked, "Excuse me?" He reiterated, "Have you rehearsed loading the helicopter?"

Still a bit confused, I inquired, "You want us to rehearse walking out to the helicopter and getting in?"

The conversation took a quick turn, "Lt. Doebler, if you feel rehearsing part of your insertion plan is beneath you, I'll happily find someone who does not feel that way and let them execute the Mission."

With that I advised my Commanding Officer we would complete the rehearsal immediately.

What can go wrong walking out to the helicopter? I felt a little silly getting the Platoon together to rehearse walking out to the helicopter. When I explained what we were doing, one of the more senior members of the Platoon remarked that he had severely sprained his ankle jogging out to the helicopter years ago and had to miss the operation. And there it was. Now I understood why the Commanding Officer didn't extend a lot of his patience with me when I questioned him about rehearsing this. There were very basic things that could go wrong and I wasn't accounting for them.

Well, what happens if someone turns their ankle and breaks it? It sounds like a silly thing to account for ... until it actually happens and I haven't accounted for it. Sure, that person obviously isn't going on the operation, but what of the skill set we've just lost? What if that operator was a sniper? Do I have another sniper going on the operation? Is the operation contingent upon sniper support? Can we conduct the operation with just one sniper team ... or no sniper teams?

Because I accounted for the potential (if however unlikely) loss of a key element of the operation, we were in a position to move forward without delay. In this case, we built in some redundancy of personnel and skill set. We were able to devise a scenario to accomplish the Mission with limited resources. Or, we could put this in as a "no-go" criterion. In other words, if this happens the operation is off.

It may be a no-go criterion because we didn't have redundancy in this particular skill set. Not ideal, but now we've at least identified a gap in our capabilities and can put together a training plan to fill this gap for future operations. All of this based on Contingency planning for walking out to the helicopter.

This level of Contingency planning, as I explained, comes with experience. Is it necessary for you to consider that somebody may choke on a banana and die at lunch time? Of course not. For now, account for Contingencies and learn. Like anything else, practice will give you clarity.

Now for the business example. I worked with a union that had to battle regularly with a very big, high profile, and powerful corporate entity. As we were working through the Planning Process, I asked the union leaders why they thought their major initiatives were stalling. Their answer was simple: on the major initiatives the powerful corporate entity would simply ignore union leadership's requests or put them off until the union stopped asking.

So, as we were identifying Actions for a particular plan we were working on, I asked about Contingencies. A couple were identified, but the obvious Contingency was eluding the union leaders. I reminded them that they just shared with me that their biggest obstacle to securing major initiatives for their union membership was that Corporate ignored them. I asked if it was likely that the same thing would happen for the initiative we were currently working on. Their answer was a definitive "Yes!" Yes, Corporate was definitely going to do what it always did and ignore them.

So, my question was simple, "What will you do when they ignore you?"

The first thing we had to do was give Corporate a time frame within which the leaders expected either a response or a meeting set to discuss the matter. Then, we went into Contingency planning based on their past experience. If management ignored them again, two days past the requested time a second email would be sent, reiterating the request and giving a new deadline. If this deadline passed, a third email would be written doing the same. If that email was ignored, an email from the union's lawyer would be sent to reiterate the request and give a new deadline, and to express concern about the lack of response from management. If the lawyer was ignored, he or she would send a second email outlining possible contractual violations to the collective bargaining agreement and possible legal recourse if the union was continuously ignored. If the union still failed to get a response, they would utilize their social media accounts and publicly highlight how they were being treated before a legal grievance was filed.

Because the union leadership had unintentionally trained Corporate to ignore them without consequence, we decided on a very patient and methodical approach to Contingencies. We anticipated that Corporate would call the union's bluff at every turn so we had to make sure that the union was willing to go the route of the most serious Contingencies of social media shaming and legal action. My very strong recommendation was not to bluff. If it meant that much to them, they should be willing to cause some discomfort and fight. If they weren't willing to go through the discomfort of social media and legal action, they should not bother making the request at all. After much discussion, they agreed it was important for many reasons and decided to execute their plan. I advised them to strap in for a bumpy ride, but I also predicted they would prevail if they followed their Contingency planning.

Sadly and predictably, Contingency after Contingency was executed. The time came for the social media campaign and legal recourse outlined by the union lawyer. The union leaders discussed abandoning the final Contingencies. After some very intense reflection, they decided to continue on with their most severe Contingencies.

In a matter of hours after the social media post went out and Corporate received the planned legal action from the union's lawyer, Corporate reached out to the union leadership. Not to capitulate, though. Corporate began to shame the union for acting so rashly. "Why in the world had they acted so childishly by posting on social media and threatening legal action?" they asked. We anticipated this response and were ready.

The union leadership unemotionally and methodically (two behavioral guidelines they adopted) outlined the very reasonable and professional steps they took to simply get a response from Corporate. The union very simply asked at that point if Corporate was ready to talk. Amazingly, they said no, they were not. They would not be bullied, they said. The legal grievance was filed as soon as the phone was hung up, and included the efforts the union went through before they finally decided to file the grievance, i.e.: their Contingency planning.

With that, Corporate was ready to talk. Much more of the same Contingency planning took place and it was painful at times, but the union leadership prevailed. It was a great moment for them and their membership.

For years, the union had been dismissing the one Contingency that was stopping them from providing big ticket items to their membership. When they realized there were a series of steps they could take to put pressure on Corporate after they'd been ignored, and then had the courage to take those steps, they began securing the initiatives that had previously stalled. Since, Contingency planning has become the lifeblood of the union's ability to deliver for their membership.

And because of their ability to use Contingency planning, the relationship between the union and Corporate moved from adversarial and transactional to collaborative and partnership-based. All because they started asking the simple question, "What will we do if …?"

SMACCC: "Communication"

The final element of SMACCC is Communication. As I've said, if you miss an element of this Planning Process you increase your likelihood for failure exponentially, so all elements are important.

However, Communication holds a sort of 1-plus status. Why? Because if we have a good Communications plan, we'll be able to quickly identify if we missed or shortchanged any of the other elements of the Planning Process.

However, if we miss or shortchange the Communications plan, then we've just inhibited our ability to quickly identify other lapses in our plan and make the necessary small adjustments in a timely fashion, rather than massive adjustments at the last second. And making massive adjustments at the last second is what happens, (only if you're lucky), when you have a poor Communications plan.

Let me break it down. If you are executing your Communications plan and ask for a status on a specific Action and you receive no response, your first question will be one of Command. "Who is in charge of that Action?" Well, you might come to realize that Command was not assigned to that Action. Fine, now you can quickly assign Command and keep rolling. However, if you didn't have a good, consistent Communications plan you wouldn't know that Action wasn't being executed until it was too late.

As the leader, you are accountable for the overall Mission. Therefore, it is incumbent upon you to know the status of the plan. To do this, you must communicate in a consistent, methodical, and precise manner.

Decide who you will talk to, when you will talk with them, how you will talk with them (i.e.: phone, in person, video conference), for how long you will talk with them, and about what you will talk with them.

The Communications plan does not refer to the soft skills of Communication like tone of voice, delivery, body language, etc. The soft skills of Communication are extremely important, but not what we are discussing.

When you are putting together your Communications plan, consider how much of what is discussed is applicable to how many people on the call. Will the information being presented on the call at any given time only be applicable to a small percentage of people on the call? If so, that is a lot of wasted time for the majority of the people. That's why we can't be lazy with our Communications plan and simply have an all hands meeting once per week.

Your rule of thumb for devising your Communications

plan should be that 100% of the information discussed on the call or meeting should be applicable to 100% of the people on the call or at the meeting.

All hands calls have their place, especially at the beginning of a Mission. It's good to let everyone know what the overall Situation and Mission are as well as a 30,000 foot view of the overall plan. But to be as efficient as possible, after that the leader should consider more targeted calls that are shorter and specific to the audience, rather than those big, unwieldy calls where people ultimately lose focus.

The next thing to consider in your Communications plan is Communication up, down, and across the chain of Command. In other words, are you sharing the progress with your boss? Are you appropriately sharing the status of the plan to those under your charge? And, are you sharing updates with those other business units that can be affected by your plan? In other words, if the success or failure of your plan can affect another business unit either positively or negatively, they need to be part of your Communications plan. This is very simply how we break down the "silos" that plague so many organizations.

Those are the six elements of SMACCC. As you can guess, there are many ways to implement SMACCC—hence, the Art of the Planning Process. We will do a deeper dive into the Art of the Planning Process and how it is used as a leadership tool in the next chapter.

So how should we begin implementing SMACCC? I recommend you start this process by simply accounting for the elements in your plan privately. Look at what you are doing, or what you want to do, and see if you have appropriately accounted for each element of SMACCC. If you have, good! Carry on! If you have not, then account for it and carry on.

As well, you can't go wrong by being very strict about the process and listing each element and then filling in the blanks. This can be a little bumpy early on until you really get the hang of it, but so is anything new that is worth doing. The key either way is to account for the elements. Have you identified the Situation? Have you identified the clear Mission? Etcetera. You'll figure out your Art of applying this Planning Process as you go and will adapt to what works best for you. Eventually your people will be in tune to the elements of the Planning Process, (whether you account for the elements strictly or not), and it will become part of the language they speak as they are making, executing, adjusting, and debriefing the plan.

I've heard, "Errol, we have a planning process. We iterate," or, "We scrum."

My response to that is, "Fantastic." But you still need to know your Mission when you scrum. You still need to identify Actions and who is in Command of which Action when you iterate. The elements of SMACCC fit into, and are essential elements, of whatever you call your Planning Process to include iterating and scrumming. Likewise with project management software. The software is not your plan or your Planning Process, it is only where you house your plan. As long as you are housing the element of SMACCC somewhere in your project management software, your plan will succeed.

Thoughts and Considerations on this "Simple" Planning Process

Remember, process is not a dirty word. The creative types out there will initially feel stifled or confined when they read through the elements of SMACCC. Not because SMACCC is stifling or confining, but because in their minds they are not separating a creative idea from the *execution* of a creative idea. Those are two different conversations.

The Navy SEALs practically invented the idea of the craziest goal—jumping out of an airplane in the middle of the night, into the middle of the ocean, with all their gear, traveling miles in the water to sneak up on and dominate an enemy that doesn't know they're coming. Does that sound like restrictive thinking? Of course not, because it isn't. We were always thinking of new and dynamic ways to do our job better.

However, when an out-of-the box, crazy idea is put on the table the next thing that happens is NOT, "Woohoo, let's go jump out of the airplane at night into the middle of the ocean right now! Let's go! Yeah!" Behind every unique and creative idea lies a disciplined and methodical Planning Process to make it come alive.

In fact, this process allows for even more creativity. Having a plan to execute a big idea is a natural stress limiter. As we've learned, when our brain is not under stress or in the fight or flight mode, we are open to new suggestions or new ideas. Yes; having a plan allows us to see from a wider lens and make necessary adjustments along the way to improve on your big idea.

For those of you who look at SMACCC and feel excited because it lays out a nice, neat place for everything and everybody, I've got some bad news for you. This won't be neat and tidy. It will be messy. Yes, the process is simple and you probably read this and thought, "Why wasn't I doing this before? I never do this, ugh! This makes so much sense!" Don't get sucked into thinking the execution of the process will be as simple as the process appears. It won't be. But that's ok, because neat and tidy isn't the goal. Mission accomplishment is the goal.

When we have a process, we are able to look back and see where things went right and where things went wrong. When we can look back with this kind of clarity, we can determine what things need to stay and what things need improvement or need to go. You may reflect on the elements of SMACCC and determine that you intuitively do most of the things already. That's fine, but operating on intuition isn't good enough. Intuition does not allow you to go back through what happened in a clear, concise, methodical fashion to unemotionally evaluate where and why things went right or wrong. Only adhering to a process does that. So if you can't seem to break through with the big idea, it's likely because you are acting on intuition alone. The Planning Process will allow you to see for yourself which of your intuitions can be trusted and which ones cannot.

As a leader you are expected to guide, train, and teach your people whenever possible and intuition cannot be taught, guided, or trained. You cannot hold people accountable to your intuition. Expectations based on intuition are not clear and do not provide for a safe, predictable environment.

You know what a leader can teach, guide, and make clear what people will be held accountable to? The elements of SMACCC.

One final note: These are the elements of a Planning Process that are used to keep people alive and achieve Mission accomplishment on the battlefield. This process was not formulated by academics in a sterile lab. It is literally born of blood. Keep an open mind when you start employing SMACCC. Account for the elements in everything you do, even if they are not applicable, which sometimes they won't be. Be patient with yourself, you'll get the hang of it with practice.

CHAPTER TWELVE

The Planning Process as a Leadership Tool

Now that we've gone through the elements of SMACCC and how to use them to make a plan that will succeed, let's discuss how the Planning Process, in conjunction with some behavioral guidelines, can be used as a leadership tool. The examples I'm going to provide are by no means the only examples of how SMACCC can be used as a leadership tool, but they are some of the most common I've come across and allow you to take the Art of the Planning Process, and your leadership effectiveness, to a whole new level.

Instilling Initiative and Autonomy: Hear the Plan First

Let's start with how SMACCC allows us to instill initiative and autonomy in our people while also giving us the ability to have a full situational awareness of overall workflow. It's the leader's job to understand the overall Situation and set the Mission, as we discussed in the last chapter.

But once we have identified and communicated the Situation and Mission, we hand over the responsibility of how that Mission will be accomplished to our people. In other words, you tell your people the Mission, and they tell you how they are going to accomplish that Mission through Actions, Command, Contingencies, and Communication. It is as simple as that. Tell them what you want them to achieve and why you want them to achieve it, and then let them get to work to figure out how they are going to do it by focusing on the elements of SMACCC.

Empowering your people in this way to act with initiative and autonomy does not mean you have no idea what your people are doing or what decisions they are making. So, when you give them the Mission and ask them to tell you how they are going to accomplish that Mission, you must hear their plan before they begin executing. That is your job as a leader; to know what your people's plan is before they begin executing. When you hear the plan before execution begins, everyone is clear under what parameters they have full authority to make decisions, or to act autonomously.

What If I Don't Like Their Plan?

The challenge for you as a leader is to understand and accept that your people may tackle an objective differently than you. This can be hard initially, but it is an absolute requirement for proper delegation. So, what happens if you, the leader, are listening to the plan and you are not comfortable with it?

Maybe you are not comfortable with the plan because it's not how you would do it so you need more convincing it will work. Or, maybe it consists of elements that, based on your experience, you are confident will not work because they have been tried before and met with failure. How do we challenge the elements of a plan as a leader while not stripping away the initiative and autonomy we are trying to create in our people?

Well, the obvious answer is that you need to ask questions. But you need to ask the right kind of questions. The most common way leaders ask questions to challenge a plan is, "Have you considered doing it this way or that way?" You may even add that it's up to them which way they decide, that you're just making a recommendation—providing food for thought. And, you may even really mean it. Or, you're hoping they'll just take the hint and do it your way. Either way, there is a serious problem with asking a question, or making a suggestion, this way.

The problem is that leaders don't make suggestions, they give orders. When you make a suggestion your employee will likely think to themselves, "Well, if I don't take the boss' suggestion and my way doesn't work that will look bad for me and I'll have to contend with some form of 'I told you so.'" So to be safe, your employee will just do it your way. Or, they may still feel strongly about doing it their way, but don't want to deal with any potential resentment or hard feelings if they come to you and say, "Thanks for your recommendation, but I'm not going to take it. I'm going to go ahead and do it my way." For the employee to deliver a message like this to the boss is easier said than done and they shouldn't be put in that position in the first place.

This simple breakdown makes it clear that this way of asking a question, or giving a suggestion, does not create or instill initiative or autonomy. It's just another form of giving an order, whether you mean it to be or not. When this happens, it's no longer their plan, now it's your plan that they are simply executing. They are not thinking or using their initiative, just executing your checklist. This doesn't create thinkers and doers who have skin in the game. It creates robots.

Challenging the Plan and Still Letting It Be Theirs

You should be able to challenge the plan. That's your job. But how do you do it in a way that keeps the plan theirs, but still challenges their thought process? Once again, SMACCC has the answer. You ask your questions, or make your challenges, in the form of Contingencies.

Let's say you are being briefed on a series of Actions and you are not comfortable with them. You see some holes. So, you simply ask, "What will you do if this thing happens?" You obviously have something in mind based on your experience, so just ask what they will do if that particular thing happens that will disrupt the Action.

One of two things will happen. First, they'll have an answer. Good! That means they are thinking and have a clear direction if that Contingency arises. It still may not be how you would do it, but now they've shown you they have thought through potential problems and have earned the opportunity to execute their way because their plan has stood up to scrutiny. And, in the process, maybe you've learned something.

The second thing that can happen is they won't have an answer. Suppose you pose the question, "What will you do if this thing happens?" and they answer with, "I don't know." Well, now you get to make recommendations or suggestions and then ask them to come back with an updated plan. You've done your job. You've appropriately imparted some of your wisdom and experience because it was solicited. You asked a question and they did not have an answer, so you provided some suggestions to kick-start their thought process.

By challenging their plan in the form of Contingency questions, you have begun to train your people to think beyond simple Actions by being aware of Contingencies. You've also allowed them to keep the plan their own by asking them to come back with an updated version. It's still their plan!

You've created thinkers because now they know you will challenge their plans through Contingency questioning. Now they will begin to think in Contingencies to challenge their own plan before they present it to you because you have made it a clear expectation, or Guideline for Behavior, that they can expect from you. That's how you develop thinkers, encourage initiative and autonomy, and make it clear what your people will be held accountable to.

I'm Afraid I'll Lose Track of What's Happening, But I Don't Want to Micromanage

How do you keep track of what's happening without micromanaging? First, let's define micromanaging. Micromanaging is giving a checklist of things to do or telling people how to do what you want them to do.

Receiving updates on what they said they were going to do is not micromanaging. Call it "microknowledging," call it whatever you want. But minimally, call it your job. It is your job to know what your people are doing and the status of the plan. How do we do this? The Communications portion of SMACCC.

When we make a Communications plan, we set the parameters for our Communication. We establish the day, time, place, topic, and length of the meeting. The first thing you've done when the parameters for your Communications plan have been set is establish what someone will be held accountable to; an update on this topic (or Action) on this date and time.

Next, you will be able to focus your conversation because you already know what you will be updated about based on the plan. "I will update you on this Action, on this day and time." Now we are not wasting time. The meeting is focused. 100% of the information being discussed is applicable to 100% of the people in the conversation.

You have now received a specific update on the plan you are overseeing. Does this sound like micromanaging? Of course it doesn't, because it's not. Having a good, consistent Communications plan allows you to stay up-to-date about what is happening without micromanaging your people.

A word of warning: If someone resists providing regular, targeted updates, or complains that you are micromanaging because you are asking for an update, you likely have a prob-

THE PLANNING PROCESS AS A LEADERSHIP TOOL | 189

lem on your hands. First because, as we have discussed, getting updates is not micromanaging. Second, who doesn't want to provide the boss with a good update? Someone who doesn't have something good to update, that's who. You may have to dive a little deeper into what this person is doing.

More Bad Questions

You've done the work as a leader. You've provided the Situation and Mission and asked for a plan to accomplish the Mission BEFORE work started. You've given your people the initiative and autonomy they crave by properly delegating the nuts and bolts of the plan to those who will be doing the work.

You've challenged their plans through Contingency questions. You have forced your people to think a couple of steps ahead in the plan and you've also taught them to do this on their own because they know you will be asking them, "What will you do if?" questions. You've developed thinkers and doers!

You are not losing track of the status of the plan because a good, consistent Communications plan was made. You are getting regular, targeted updates. You are not wasting your people's time because 100% of the information on your calls is applicable to 100% of the people on the call.

And after all this great leadership work, you do this: "Let me know if you need anything!"

Or you might ask, "What can I do to help?"

Your intentions are good, but this stands out like a sore thumb compared to all the good leadership work done up until this point. The purpose of all the work up to this point is so you, the leader, can actually identify specifically where you can help by asking questions around the topic of the scheduled Communication. What do I mean?

If there is an Action, we know from the last chapter that that Action should have a date it will be completed by. One of the obvious areas of discussion during your update is whether or not that Action will be completed on schedule. If it is clear the answer is yes, then your employee probably doesn't need any help with anything right now. Good! Tell them, "Great work!" and let them be on their way.

If the answer is, "No, we're going to be late," the obvious question for the leader to ask is "Why?" Ask, "Why?" and then listen.

For example, you ask, "Why?" and your employee tells you that the Action will not be completed on time because it is simply taking longer than expected. That's fine, it happens.

Then perhaps they go on to tell you that everyone is working overtime and the Action will only be a week late. "We'll get it done, don't worry."

As a leader, you should be proud of that reaction. It's "can do." It's ownership. It's all good. But maybe your employee is so focused on getting the job done they are not clearly identifying areas where they need help. But you, the leader, can.

This is where the Communications plan has become a leadership tool by identifying where your people need help. "The task is just taking longer than we expected, but we'll work overtime to get it done." I, as the leader, love the spirit, but as we discussed in Cultural Awareness and Recognition, that is not a sustainable solution. Is "working overtime to get it done" a sustainable and transferable behavior that you want to make up your culture? It's only important to go the "extra mile" and "buckle down" and show "grit" when it's important to show those things, which should only be sparingly. If that is how you are constantly doing business, then there is a problem.

Are you helping your employee if your response to them is, "OK, just tell me what you need?" I don't think so. There are a couple of other obvious, more targeted, questions you could ask that would likely drill down on a more specific cause to the delay in question. "Do you need more resources? Will another person help?" "Are you getting the support from the other business units that was promised?" "Are there gaps in skill set or training that are slowing you down?"

The point is that a good, consistent Communications plan should allow the leader to ask targeted questions about the status of the Mission, identify problems before they become too big, and provide the necessary assistance or solution when the employee may not see it. If your go-to as a leader is, "Just let me know what you need," then you are either not listening to the updates or they are not being held consistently enough for you to have a firm grasp on the big picture.

It's Their Plan, Shouldn't They See the Problems?

As we continue with our example, it begs the question, "Why won't they see the cause for delay? It's their plan, shouldn't they know why it is stalling?" They may not see it, or claim to not see it, for a lot of reasons. Maybe they are ashamed or hesitant to ask for help because you might think they are not capable if they ask for more resources. Maybe they don't have enough experience to even know what to ask for. Maybe they have lost the forest through the trees and cannot see the obvious. That is why asking, "Is there anything you need?" or stating something grand, but ultimately meaningless like, "Just tell me what you need" is not what leaders should be doing. Your people may not know what they need.

Get a clear and concise update based on the Communication portion of the plan and you'll see what the challenges are or where your people need assistance. That's what leaders do. They see the problems before they become unmanageable and help make the small adjustments early. This is to say nothing of the fact that you are giving your people the personal and targeted attention that builds real human connection. Leaders do this by focusing on the Communications plan and using SMACCC as a leadership tool.

SMACCC and Finding Calm Amidst the Chaos

Let's now move to how SMACCC can limit anxiety and allow you to perform in a calm and clear manner under stress. More often than not, stress and anxiety are caused by uncertainty or the feeling that things are out of control. Or more specifically, out of *our* control.

We very often experience this stress and anxiety because we simply don't know how things are going to turn out. There is enough uncertainty to go around, so we should take every opportunity to create certainty where we can. How do we do that? By having a plan.

If we follow the elements of SMACCC, when chaos ensues we can go back to our Mission and ask ourselves, "Ok, things seem a little out of control. What are we actually trying to achieve?" When we do that ... when we remind ourselves what our Mission is, we can evaluate what Actions people are taking and determine if they drive Mission accomplishment. If they don't, you as the leader can begin refocusing people's Actions. If they do ... well then there is nothing to worry about because people are acting towards Mission accomplishment. We've created certainty by knowing what people should be doing based on the clearly identified Mission. Common sense, but not always common practice.

A good example of limiting anxiety through the use of SMACCC is deadline management. Deadlines should never sneak up on a leader because the leader should already know the status of everyone's work. How? Because the leader has implemented and followed an effective Communications plan. With an effective Communications plan, the leader is getting regular, concise updates from their people. So, a week out from any deadline, a leader should already know if the project will meet, be ahead, or be behind the deadline date. When you already know the outcome of something and can communicate "Why?" to the applicable parties ahead of time (like your own boss), there is nothing to be anxious about.

Even in the "worst case" scenario of being late to the deadline, if you communicate and are aware ahead of time you will be behind schedule, then that means you've also done the work of understanding why you are behind schedule. You can make the necessary adjustments and communicate this "bad news" unemotionally, methodically, and with confidence.

But It's Not Always That Cut and Dry

So, having a plan ahead of time creates certainty, and certainty in and of itself is a stress limiter. But what about those times when a real emergency arises? When something serious and truly unexpected thrusts itself upon you and your team? How do you handle these Situations with the calm and confidence of a leader? It may not be something you planned for, but that's ok, because you know HOW to make a plan.

In moments of stress, we default to what we know. We go to the behaviors that have been ingrained in our brain and are habit. So, this begs the question: What do you know? Some people know panic. Some people know blame. Some people know retreat. Some people know excuses. What should you know? Know a Planning Process, know SMACCC. Knowing a Planning Process allows you to take the emotion out of an otherwise emotional Situation.

In the first element of the leadership process, Emotional Awareness and Recognition, we talked about the non-leader-ship process of Action: TRIGGER to EMOTION directly to ACTION. Then we discussed needing to add THINK and DE-CIDE to change the leadership thought process to TRIGGER to EMOTION to THINK/DECIDE to ACTION. That's all well and good, as long as you know what to do inside of THINK and DECIDE. What should you do inside of THINK and DE-CIDE? Have a plan! Go through SMACCC.

Here is a combat example to bring this point home—the first time I was shot at in Afghanistan. Obviously, the trigger is getting shot at. I felt many emotions at that moment, which was fine. We don't limit ourselves to one emotion because we can have several competing emotions at the same time.

I felt a rush of excitement and exhilaration. I also felt surprise and the obvious rush of fear. That was no time to hope my Actions were appropriate. In that instance, I had to know what my Actions were going to be or else I'd suffer the worst of all consequences, Mission failure, injury, or death. All unacceptable.

So, TRIGGER, getting shot at. EMOTION, excitement, fear, surprise, exhilaration. I then went immediately to THINK and DECIDE … SMACCC. The SITUATION was this: I was getting shot at and the rush of emotions and adrenaline through my body were about to make me fall down and relinquish my responsibilities in the patrol—a deadly proposition for those who were counting on me to do my job and watch their back. Did this fit the SITUATION fact check? Is your response to this, "Well, what did you do about that?" You bet your ass it did! I was able to define the SITUATION clearly. Good start!

My MISSION was simple: Physically get control of myself so I could carry out my duties.

My ACTIONS were simple: Acknowledge the impact my emotions were having on what was happening. This allowed me to understand that the sudden onset of all those emotions created an adrenaline rush in my body that temporarily weakened my legs, better known as an adrenaline dump. Having that in my conscious mind allowed me to avoid dwelling on it and focus on my next ACTIONS: Identify where the shots were coming from, identify my field of fire, locate a target, locate the other members of the patrol. In short, get back to the standard operating procedures associated with being shot at and not let external circumstances control how I responded.

My CONTINGENCIES were also simple: If I succumbed to the adrenaline dump and fell, I would simply get back up. Is that common sense? Of course it was. But remember, we were dealing with a high stress, life-and-death Situation that could easily cloud any rational thought. Because I was going through that process, falling would not have fazed me in the least because I was fully aware of everything that was happening and why it was happening. I did not have the added stress of the unknown, I went exactly to what I knew. And on the SMACCC process went ...

The point is, I went to what I knew in a true moment of crisis and was able to do it quickly and with clarity. Because I made a habit of Emotional Awareness and Recognition and had control of my Actions by employing SMACCC inside of THINK and DECIDE, I was able to act professionally and calmly during a true moment of stress and danger. I was able to use the SMACCC we had planned before the incident, and I was able to enact a new SMACCC in the midst of it.

Of course, moments of stress and danger will vary from the battlefield to the boardroom, to the kitchen table. But the process for remaining and acting calm under stress is the same: Know a Planning Process, make a plan, and execute that plan. Go to what you know and know a Planning Process. Know SMACCC to stay calm amidst the chaos.

CHAPTER THIRTEEN

SMACCC! Your Brain Is Paying Attention; Rewiring and Prioritizing

YOU'RE SITTING ON THE COUCH WATCHING AMERICAN Gangster for the umpteenth time, eating chicken wings and chips and salsa. The last time you watched it you drank a few too many Budweisers, so today you are going to go with Bud Light or Coke. As you are enjoying the movie (again), you realize it's been a while since you did any exercise. Actually, you realize it's been a while since you read a book, went to a museum, or did anything on your free time other than watch American Gangster and eat crappy food.

This makes you feel a little bad. You are not proud of yourself. So, you boldly proclaim (to yourself) that you are going to change … tomorrow! Then you throw another chicken wing to the back of your throat as you contemplate how great tomorrow will look. But you don't want to contemplate it too much because the good part of the movie is coming up.

Do you know what your brain is doing at that moment? Laughing at you. That's not the scientific term, but it might as well be. Your brain knows you are not serious because your Actions did not even come close to your "conviction." You said something and just sat there doing the same old thing. Your brain did not create any new chemicals because no new emotion was created. No new chemicals were sent to the body from the brain because no new Action was taken to create a new experience which creates new emotions. Tomorrow will look just like today, count on it.

But, you can play out the same scenario with a twist: This time instead of just sitting there doing the same thing (because you are going to start tomorrow), you start to make a plan. Instead of throwing the next chicken wing to the back of your throat, you put it down and focus on making a plan for how you're going to begin turning your life around.

Do you know what your brain is doing now? It's paying attention. Why is it paying attention? Because this is a new experience. As you go through the elements of the Planning Process your brain is creating new synaptic connections and sending new chemicals to the body. You are literally changing the physiology of your mind and your body by making a plan.

You write your plan down according to the elements of SMACCC. You can now see your purpose (Situation) and focus (Mission). Because we have purpose and focus our brain is less scattered. We know from previous chapters that when our brain is less scattered and more focused it relaxes. When the brain relaxes it opens your ability to see things from a broader perspective and be more creative.

When your brain is relaxed and more creative, you can practice metacognition. You are aware of what you are doing and what you are feeling.[77] Because you are practicing meta-cognition, or being in the moment, you are aware of when you are not executing the Actions in your plan and you can quickly move back to them so you never get too far off course. You are creating a new mind because you are following your plan.

As you focus on your plan, you begin to see in your mind what you want to achieve. When you see what you want to achieve you become happy, content, and inspired. You are now creating a new chemical reality in your body and mind based on these new emotions. And they are elevated emotions! Not the old ugly emotions of hidden guilt, shame, and worthless-ness you were feeling but suppressing while sitting on the couch, watching television and eating junk food.

You run into a stumbling block as you are performing the Actions to your plan. But instead of stressing out and quitting, you readjust because you've accounted for some of the predict-able stumbles you might face along the way (Contingencies). Because of this, you are quickly back on track. Your brain con-tinues to change as it adapts to your new Actions. It starts to strengthen those synaptic connections in your brain based on your new behaviors, thoughts, and emotions.

You are following your plan, making necessary adjustments along the way, and you are making progress. You begin to focus on how you are feeling now and how you will feel in the future. These, once again, are elevated emotions. The ones that up-regulate our genes and make us healthy. And now you have begun to flip the script on those past, negative emotions and thoughts that you've repeated over and over again. The ones that science tells us down-regulate our genes and make us sick.[78]

Now instead of dwelling on a negative emotion of the past (worthlessness and guilt for your past behaviors?) and allowing those negative emotions to dominate your present and future thinking (like we know they will), you are allowing the positive emotions of the future to dominate your present and future thinking. Now your behavioral change takes another sharp turn for the positive because your brain and body are now becoming neurochemically addicted to THESE behaviors and thoughts.

When we make a plan, we are signaling to our brain we are serious, and it reacts in kind as I just described. These are broad strokes of science, but they are accurate and show the power of planning from a scientific view, in case you hadn't already bought in.

Practicing the Art with Cold Exposure

As you've noticed, we can practice the Art of each element of the leadership process with cold exposure. The difference is the intention we put behind each practice session in the cold. Again, another Guideline for Behavior to practice with cold exposure is Acting with intention. If you did everything with clear intention, would you get better? Of course you would! That makes Acting with intention a good Guideline for Behavior to consider.

So, what is our intention stepping into the cold as it relates to SMACCC? Cold exposure is a tool to help you consider the elements of SMACCC as a matter of course and habit in your day-to-day. This is so important because as you get good at this you will realize that the need for considering the elements of SMACCC are everywhere in our lives.

Let's look at how applying SMACCC to an ice bath might work to help you get into the rhythm of SMACCC:

Situation. (Set of circumstances dictating the need for Action): The Planning Process is new to me and I want to be able to seamlessly integrate it into my leadership skills.

Mission. (Your goal or what you want to accomplish): To consciously cover each one of the elements of SMACCC before, during, and after the ice bath.

Actions (The things you will do to accomplish your Mission):
1. Identify my emotions before I enter the ice bath.
2. Exercise THINK/DECIDE as part of the TRIGGER to EMOTION to THINK/DECIDE to ACT.
3. Determine how I want to behave (Guidelines for Behavior) when I consider THINK/DECIDE. I.E.: I want to act professionally and not show excessive and unnecessary emotional responses. I want to show courage and move to getting in the ice bath quickly without procrastination.

4. Enter the ice bath in a calm, methodical fashion.

5. Recognize the fight or flight response (Sympathetic Nervous System) as I get in the water (breath being taken away) and remember this is a normal response.

6. Find my breath through a purposeful exhale which will serve to calm me down by activating the vagus nerve. Continue to focus only on my breath by breathing in through my nose and exhaling either through my nose or mouth, eventually getting to a long, gentle nasal breathing pattern.

7. Focus my attention on my breath. When my mind wanders to external thoughts like how cold the water is, or how much longer I should stay in, or how much I hate this, bring my mind back to my breath.

8. Once I find and maintain my breath through a long, gentle breathing pattern, exit the ice bath in a calm, methodical manner.

9. Once out, take the horse stance position (deep bend at the knees, wide stance) and move my upper body and arms from side to side to begin to warm myself in space. Maintain a strict focus on this movement and when my mind wanders to an external thought (I need to get a towel and sweatshirt!) bring my mind back to my breath and movement.

Contingencies. (Consider things that can go wrong as I execute Actions and account for them):

1. I feel the need to immediately exit the water or make some overly dramatic gesture like yelling "Oh, shit,

this is cold!": I will remind myself that this type of re-action is normal, re-focus on finding my breath and behaving in a professional and courageous manner.

2. I struggle to calm my breathing down: I will contin-ue to act with professionalism and courage and not succumb to the urge to exit the ice. I will exaggerate my exhale to force the activation of my vagus nerve to calm myself down. When my mind wanders from my breath, I will bring focus back to it. If necessary, I will exit the ice bath, refocus on my plan, and try it again.

3. The pain in my fingers and toes becomes unbearable even though I have found my breath and am other-wise remaining calm amidst the chaos of the ice bath: I will understand that this is nothing more than an en-vironmental response to the cold called vasoconstric-tion. Since I am new to ice baths and have successfully found my breath and calm, I will simply end the ice bath because there is no reason to endure unnecessary pain. As I grow more experienced, I know my body will eventually adapt and the pain will subside and I will begin to endure small amounts of discomfort a lit-tle at a time until I have found the ability to seamlessly adapt to this response with little to no discomfort.

Command. I and I alone am in Command of my Actions. Out-side influences or thoughts have nothing to do with my ability to execute on my Actions to achieve my Mission.

Communication. I will check in with my breathing and focus continuously by practicing metacognition. I will check in with myself constantly to ensure I am aware of what I am doing and aware of what I am feeling. (Or, this section could be "not applicable." It doesn't matter, as long as you have accounted for it.)

If you make this plan BEFORE you get into the ice bath your chances of achieving all the things you want to achieve are undeniably excellent!

Bringing It Into the Office

To begin getting the hang of the Planning Process consider past, present, and future initiatives.

Past: Recall an initiative that met with substandard results, straight failure, or stagnation. Now go through the elements of SMACCC and see if one was not accounted for and how this affected the overall progress on the initiative. Get ready for some scary revelations.

Present: Every day identify at least one of the elements of SMACCC you are executing on a current project. Perhaps you re-defined or clarified an overall Mission. Perhaps you are executing part of your Communications plan by getting an update from a subordinate or are updating another business unit yourself. The point of this is simple: if you can't identify that the Actions you are taking throughout the day are contributing to Mission success, then you'll need to re-evaluate what you and your team are actually doing. This may end up being a painful drill, but it will make clear very quickly how targeted your and your team's workflow is.

Future: Think ahead to initiatives that are being considered or are on the board for future execution. Go through each element of SMACCC and consider how thoroughly each has been considered, especially Situation and Mission. Consider resources available for Command to undertake the Actions necessary for Mission accomplishment. Consider the Situation. Do you know why the initiative is being undertaken? If you know why, does it merit Action now or can it wait?

This is an excellent way to become accustomed to SMACCC. You'll be less emotionally attached to a past objective that may not have gone as you would have liked, and you'll be able to clearly assess what elements of SMACCC you may have missed or short-changed. This will give you great awareness of what is currently happening in a project, so you can make your necessary adjustments. Finally, you'll be in a great position to have a full plan in place for your future project and you'll start to see the benefits of planning before you Act.

SMACCC and Prioritization

Let's now address prioritization and how SMACCC, combined with proper behavioral guidelines, can help with this leadership challenge. Everybody is busy, there's a lot to do and not enough time to do it. What happens so often is we end up with what seems like 100 things going on at once. So, we write a to-do list and try to knock out a little on each task every day.

This makes us feel good. We are working hard on all our responsibilities. But, if you look at it closer, it's a losing proposition. Why? Because responsibilities keep getting added. So, if you are working on them all a little at a time, how can we expect to get any of them fully completed?

The more this pattern happens, the more it seems like all you are doing is putting out fires because you are continuously adding things to your to-do list without actually knocking any of them off. That feeling of putting out fires all day every day comes down to prioritization.

Let's say, based on the challenge of properly prioritizing, we adopt a behavior guideline that's part of Navy SEAL combat ethos to prioritize and execute. (I like to add Prioritize and Execute to Completion). Remember, If we didn't change the way we made, marketed, or sold our widget, but behaved in these ways, would we get better? If we prioritized and executed to completion, would this make us better? Of course, so that makes it a good behavioral guideline. But, HOW do we prioritize?

This is where SMACCC helps us. First, identify the Situation for each project or task you are working on or need to work on. The Situation ... the set of circumstances dictating a need for Action.

Let's say your SEAL patrol gets ambushed and one or more of your teammates has been shot and needs assistance. You've got two Situations at play here. First, you've been ambushed.

The enemy has located you, got the drop on you, and is shooting at you. Second, you have operators down and injured. Without the proper medical assistance, they will die.

Combat is the ultimate expression of consequence. And in this instance, if the leader doesn't correctly prioritize which Situation they will act on first, the ultimate consequences will be realized: Mission failure, more injury, or death. All unacceptable.

Both Situations are dire, and both need to be addressed as soon as possible. The first challenge is to realize you have two Situations at play that will require separate Missions. We need to fight back and we need to save our teammates' lives. But if we try to do them both at the same time, we will lose the fight, lose the lives of those who are already injured, and likely get more people killed. That lesson has been learned in blood—hence the combat ethos—or behavior, to prioritize and execute to completion.

Given the two Situations and their corresponding Missions, we must now unemotionally and methodically decide which one needs to be prioritized. Unemotional and methodical, by the way, another behavior that makes us better, especially in this example.

We love our teammates and every instinct in our fiber tells us to go to them immediately and save their lives. However, the incoming fire from our adversary is the priority. Because if we don't suppress the fire from the enemy we will continue to take casualties and lose lives. So, as distasteful as it seems, we must prioritize and first engage the enemy and suppress their fire before we move to help our teammates.

In this example, the behavior of prioritize and execute sets us on the right path. We follow SMACCC, identify the importance of the Situations and Missions in play, and use an unemotional and methodical behavior to properly prioritize and begin executing. How do we execute? Continue to follow the elements of SMACCC—it's nothing more than a plan we need to execute. And the elements of SMACCC allow us to execute any plan, any time.

The key here is that we could not have possibly prioritized if we did not identify and separate the multiple Situations and Missions in play. While combat highlights the importance of following the leadership process, let's once again bring it back to the boardroom.

In our combat example, we are forced to prioritize suppressing the enemy fire over coming to the aid of our teammates while we listen to their pleas of, "Help me! Help me!" If we can prioritize over those human pleas, which we can, we can surely handle the indignation someone at the office may feel when we ask them "Why?" or "What's the Situation?" in order to properly assess and effectively prioritize their request for something to be done immediately.

Our injured teammates in my combat example know we must suppress enemy fire first. They know we must prioritize and execute before we move on to the next task of saving their lives. It doesn't mean they don't still beg you to make an exception. But, they know HOW WE DO BUSINESS! They know the established Guidelines for Behavior. They know their teammates are acting with Emotional Awareness and Recognition so they can act in the overall best interest of the group. They know we are following the elements of SMACCC so we will get to them as fast as possible.

If following the elements of SMACCC is good enough to save lives and find victory on the battlefield, it's good enough to consider for your team. Make identifying the Situation and properly prioritizing based on the Situation and Mission the way your team does business and you will be relieved of the daily fires we use as an excuse to underperform from day to day.

The Challenge of Technology and Prioritization

If you are in the world of technology this scenario should sound familiar to you. I have come across it countless times working with technology companies and technology engineers.

You are the leader of a software engineering team. You have just been advised that there is a new customer ready to sign a large contract and several existing customers ready to not only renew, but to expand their current contracts.

Typically, there are several new features the clients want built into the platform before the deals are finalized. You are getting pressure from every angle to incorporate the new features immediately so the deals can be closed and the company can realize their end-of-the-year revenue goals. Without the deals, the company will fall short of its year-end projections. However, your platform has become unstable and will not likely be able to support the new features for an acceptable amount of time.

Again, you have a few Situations at play here. New business and current contracts are being renewed and expanded as long as new features are added to the platform. Meeting year-end earnings goals is contingent upon these deals being closed immediately. Your platform is currently unstable, and you are not sure how well it can support the new, required features.

You get the point. Here we can identify three separate Situations at play and decide which one needs to be handled first. This is a sticky scenario, but a common one. As you prioritize based on the competing Situations, you can clearly identify your Missions and the remaining portions of the plan. Very likely you will need to stabilize your platform first and foremost (at least that has been the most successful path I've seen taken in these scenarios). If that is your top priority, then the Communication aspect of your plan, as is usually the case, becomes all the more important. You've got to explain that the features your customers desire can't be added until the platform is stabilized.

Not the best news, but when it's communicated in an honest, logical, organized, and unemotional fashion to the client the chances are you've just increased your trust level with them. And you've done this because you prioritized based on competing, but clearly identified, Situations. This is how a leader uses SMACCC to prioritize and make the best decisions for their clients, team, and organization.

Big Picture Prioritization and Biting Off More Than You Can Chew

SMACCC makes clear what the required elements of a good plan are. So, when we make a plan, we are identifying the resources we will use and the timeline we will be following. As you've seen, a good plan takes a lot of work. It can use a lot of resources and take more time than we anticipated.

When we are asked to tackle another task and begin that Planning Process immediately, we must run it up against the plan that is already in motion. Do we have the time and the resources to undergo two tasks simultaneously? If you do, go for it. If you don't, you have a decision to make. You now must prioritize which project you will focus on based on the knowledge that you can't effectively focus on two at the same time because of limited resources, limited time, limited budget or all three.

The number of projects running simultaneously can be four or five depending on the size of your organization, but the point remains the same. SMACCC shows you the resources and time it will take to complete a Mission, and this will make it clear that prioritization is not only important, it's a requirement of ongoing Mission accomplishment. And Mission accomplishment is what is expected of leaders.

Let the plans show how many things can be done at once. Then, prioritization simply becomes a matter of course if you are paying attention to SMACCC.

Meeting Focus and Disputes

Meetings are a challenge for even the best run organizations. Maybe you are having too many meetings. Perhaps the meetings last too long. Is 100% of the content being presented in the meeting applicable to 100% of the people in the meeting?

Can you walk out of your meetings and clearly articulate why the meeting was being held, what the goal of the meeting was, and if it was accomplished? Did the meeting stay on point or move from topic to topic like shifting winds?

Having an agenda for a meeting is an excellent place to start, but it's not enough because discussion on a particular agenda item can still be unwieldy or unfocused. As the leader, it is your job to ensure that projects move toward Mission accomplishment. Therefore, the topics covered during a meeting and the questions you ask during a meeting are critical.

Remember, you can't hold people accountable if they don't know what they are supposed to be accountable to. When people know what they are supposed to be accountable to, it creates a predictable environment. There is enough unpredictability to go around. Let's create the predictability where we can because when we do that, we'll be better equipped to handle the unpredictability that will inevitably find us.

So, what should we hold people accountable to during meetings? Why not the elements of SMACCC? If these are the elements that make a successful plan, why wouldn't they be the elements people are required to address during a meeting? If people knew they were going to be accountable to the elements of SMACCC during the meeting and they addressed those elements, would the meeting run more efficiently with the most important elements of the plan covered? Would you cover more in less time? Yes, you would.

I presented this concept to a leadership team who was struggling with their meetings. One of my first orders of business with this client was to sit in on their weekly meetings. They were usually scheduled for an hour but always went at least twice as long. Furthermore, what had actually been accomplished during the meeting was difficult to discern.

As a fix (in addition to an actual meeting agenda) we put forward that nobody could speak unless it addressed one of the elements of SMACCC. It was an initially painful process as it seemed I was doing most of the talking early on by interrupting and asking which element of SMACCC was being addressed. It was clear to everyone that the meetings were essentially free-for-alls with everyone just sounding off with random thoughts and opinions.

However, with a little guidance and discipline, it was only a few weeks until the meetings were highly productive, professional, and short. All because we kept the discussion limited to only the most essential elements that everyone knew they would be held accountable to, those of SMACCC.

What of disputes during meetings, whether the meetings are informal or formal? If you've ever really listened to a dispute, you'll find that the parties involved are often not even talking about the same thing. They are just trying to get their points or opinions across, or they're finger pointing. Sound familiar?

How does a leader get people back on point and focused? By asking two simple questions: "Why are we here?" Situation. And, "What are we trying to accomplish?" Mission. When I say ask two simple questions, I mean actually ask them. And don't ask the questions rhetorically. Wait for an answer. What you will likely find is that the parties arguing don't have the

214 | THE PROCESS, ART, AND SCIENCE OF LEADERSHIP

same answers to those questions. And if they don't have the same answers to those very basic, operational questions, then that means they are having an argument about different things.

It's very tough to settle a dispute when the people involved are talking about different things. Get alignment and agreement on the Situation and Mission and the disputes will move very quickly to problem solving. When the leader gets alignment on Situation and Mission, they can bring the conversation back to a specific place when it begins to veer off course, which it will.

When someone purposely or un-purposely brings up a point, however valid, that is not in alignment with the clearly identified Situation or Mission, the leader can easily and appropriately redirect by saying something to the effect of, "Valid point. But that's a different conversation. Let's stay focused on this Situation and Mission." They may not like having their amazing point turned away, but they will know "why" and that the "why" makes sense.

Try this for meetings, whether it's a team meeting, a leadership meeting, or maybe you've joined a board of directors and you're figuring out how to add value: Write down the elements of SMACCC, Situation, Mission, Actions, Command, Contingencies, Communication, and put them in front of you during meetings. Check off the element when it has been covered during the meeting. If you haven't heard an element covered, ask yourself if it is applicable or not. A word of caution, you may find this drill disturbing initially because so many of the elements of SMACCC won't be covered.

To add real value, when you see an element of SMACCC has not been covered, chime in with, "I'm sorry, but I wasn't clear on who was overall in charge of this initiative." Or, "This sounds great, but I'm not clear on what the specific goal is. Can we clarify exactly what we are trying to accomplish?" When we keep the questions simple and focus on the important elements of a plan, SMACCC, the impact will be profound and often (silently) deafening.

So, again, leaders keep focus on Mission accomplishment and know what questions to ask. During meetings, the elements of SMACCC will keep you Mission-focused and will give you a guide as to what questions to ask to fill in gaps. It will also allow you to diffuse and appropriately redirect confrontations. This is how leaders manage meetings.

Put it to Work

Practice this concept every day! Everyday identify how you used SMACCC as a leadership tool. How did you ask questions? How did you redirect poor behavior? How did you remain calm under stressful Situations? The most common problems we face every day can be brought back to incorporating SMACCC into every aspect of our lives. Use SMACCC and change how your brain is rewired. Use SMACCC and change your neurochemical makeup. Use SMACCC and have an understanding of why things went wrong in the past so you can avoid the same mistakes in the future.

Now go make a plan and execute towards Mission accomplishment, because that's what leaders do!

CHAPTER FOURTEEN

Element Five— Facing the Resistance

GREAT LEADERSHIP IS ABOUT SOMETHING BIGGER THAN yourself, and it doesn't matter who, where, or what you are leading. The Process, Art, and Science of Leadership is a common sense approach that is easy to understand. Follow it and you will find success as a leader in every aspect of your life.

By now you've seen that implementing the process of great leadership is hard. It requires a consistent and focused humility and discipline. And even with this humility and discipline in place we stumble. There always seems to be something lurking around the corner that is trying to derail our ability to accomplish something bigger than ourselves.

In the final Element of the leadership process, we're going to look at that "something" that works doggedly to subvert our leadership efforts and, for that matter, our efforts to become better human beings. That something is the "Resistance."[79] Its definition is: "The refusal to accept or comply with something; the attempt to prevent something by Action or argument." For our purposes, we'll further define the "Resistance" as that unexplained force of nature that works to stop you from accomplishing something bigger than yourself. Which is what leadership is; something bigger than yourself.

For example, the Resistance does not show itself when you are happily eating greasy takeout food on the couch while you binge-watch the latest iteration of junk TV. The Resistance feeds that behavior.

But you will find the Resistance sitting on the same couch, but this time deciding to watch an educational documentary and eat non-processed, heart healthy organic food. When you begin trying to make positive changes in your life you can always count on the Resistance showing itself.

What's another example? Well, the Resistance won't show itself when you are firmly planted inside a group of people and participating in bad-mouthing or gossiping about someone else. And, of course, that someone is not in earshot. The Resistance feeds that behavior.

But, you are likely to come across the Resistance if inside that same group of people you don't participate in the bad-mouthing or gossip. Or even more antagonizing towards the Resistance, you walk away or speak out against this abhorrent behavior. The Resistance cannot tolerate that behavior and will make a strong showing either within yourself, every-

ELEMENT FIVE–FACING THE RESISTANCE | 219

where else, or both. Because that's where the Resistance lives, within yourself and everywhere else.

The Resistance will take many forms when it shows itself: uncertainty, fear, ego, jealousy, anger, procrastination, judgement, self-doubt, laziness. The number of ways the Resistance can take hold seem endless.

The leadership process is common sense so it's hard to reject the validity of the process. It makes a positive impact on the individual and collectively as it calls for people to raise their level of consciousness; as teams, as leaders, as human beings. Yet, despite its common sense and effectiveness, people will resist it. You will resist it at times. Why? Because it calls for higher awareness, reflection, and positive Action. The very things the Resistance refuses to tolerate.

As long as you are trying to achieve excellence, the Resistance will never go away. The Resistance is an ongoing Contingency that you, the leader, should always expect and account for. We know that people are going to naturally resist something that is unfamiliar to them because they have already neurochemically conditioned themselves to a particular behavior based on past emotions they keep reliving.[80]

So, when you begin to implement Guidelines for Behavior or SMACCC, it will be unfamiliar to your people. They will resist. What does this knowledge do for us as leaders? It gives us awareness, so we don't need to take the inevitable resistance personally, because it's very likely not personal. It's a neurochemical addiction.

When the Resistance Hits the Team

It's one thing to combat the Resistance using the leadership process for our own inner demons. But what about when the Resistance infiltrates your team? What then? It's the same answer: go back to the process.

When a member or members of your team are hit with the Resistance, you'll feel something; you'll have an emotion. You'll recognize something isn't right. Maybe in this instance you are feeling insecure or unsure of yourself as a leader because your plan or overall process is facing Resistance. Simply paint by numbers: identify your emotions, go through TRIGGER to EMOTION to THINK/DECIDE to ACTION. Inside of THINK and DECIDE employ SMACCC and review if what you are doing is consistent with the team's Guidelines for Behavior.

When the Resistance hits your team, as it inevitably will, check yourself first inside all the elements of the leadership process. If you missed something the process will tell you and you can make the adjustments. If you haven't missed anything, it will be time for the next step. But for now, check yourself. Here's what your internal SMACCC dialogue might look like:

- *Situation:* The Resistance is speaking to my team in "this" way.

- *Mission:* Ensure the directions you provided to the team are clear, fair, and reasonable. Have you followed the leadership process and made clear what everyone will be held accountable to?

■ *Actions:*

- Review the Guidelines for Behavior. Have you made clear what behaviors your team will be held accountable to?
- Have you consistently reviewed the Guidelines for Behavior regularly and are you having people answer for them when they are not followed?
- Review the plan for the current initiative and ensure you have accounted for all the elements of SMACCC.
- Review your recent Actions. Have they been driven by emotions or have you been making conscious decisions based on your emotions?

■ *Contingencies:*

- You find some holes in the plan because you missed an element of SMACCC or never clearly identified a behavior you were expecting from everyone. Good! Now you know the Resistance is likely coming from an unclear plan or behavioral guideline, so the team is acting out of sorts. You'll make the proper adjustments, Communicate them to the team, and move forward.
- You make the adjustments and the Resistance persists. That's ok, because you've checked SMACCC and covered all the elements. The plan is solid. You've reiterated your behavioral guidelines and ensured everyone was clear on them and in agreement. Now you must be patient and courageous and trust the process. It's just the Resistance talking to your team. But, you always

account for the Resistance as a running Contingency and you know the process can beat the Resistance. So, you press on unemotionally and methodically.

- **Command:** You are in Command! You are the leader and you are in charge of your decisions and Actions ... not the fear and chaos the Resistance is trying to create.

- **Communication:** How will you communicate to the team? With consistency and confidence because you know you have put the right thought into your decisions and Actions because you have covered all the elements of the process.

We use SMACCC to fight the Resistance towards the process. Now everything should be alright, right? Well, I hate to break it to you, but despite your best efforts some of your people may lose the battle with the Resistance. So now what do you do?

Moving from Accountability to Consequence

This is where we move from accountability to consequence. Remember, accountability is not a bad word. It's simply asking someone to account for their Actions. It doesn't matter if the answer is good, bad, or somewhere in the middle. If you've asked the question and received an answer, you've held someone accountable. And, if you've followed the elements of the process, then you will have made clear WHAT people are being held accountable to.

Likewise, if you've made clear what people are being held accountable to, you've also reiterated these expectations on a consistent basis. OK; let's break this accountability-to-consequence thing down from the beginning as it relates to your people losing the battle to the Resistance.

You've worked the leadership process. You've become situationally aware of emotions and what your team does by practicing Emotional and Cultural Awareness and Recognition. Since you're now fully aware and in tune to your surroundings, you are able to identify Guidelines for Behavior that will define your culture and make you and your team better.

You also know that for the Guidelines for Behavior to stick, you must reiterate them consistently and on a regular basis, so your team is aware of their importance. There is no question at this point that your Guidelines for Behavior are how your team does business.

You are also conscious that for projects to succeed, it is critical to follow the elements of SMACCC. By following the elements of SMACCC and making your team aware that they will be accountable to these elements of the Planning Process, you've added another layer of clarity regarding their accountability.

As you battle small bouts of Resistance through the process, which is normal, you go about the business of making small corrections where necessary. You can easily do this because people are fully aware of what they are being held accountable to and a simple reminder of "that's not how we do business here" is all that's required to keep the momentum going. Because the Resistance is a running Contingency for you, you are always on the lookout for it and ready to battle it unemotionally and methodically.

In short, when there is a misstep, you don't go directly to consequence. You go to accountability first by asking them to explain their Actions and refocusing them on what they are being held accountable to. Because the environment you've created is clear and predictable, and everyone is speaking the same leadership language, people like coming to work and the team morale is high.

Except for that one person who is not responding to proper accountability. So, like a good leader, you've checked your process to ensure that this one person's Resistance is not because of a misstep you've made. You ensure that this person's roles and responsibilities inside of the plans they have been a part of have been clear. You've ensured you've held them accountable by asking them "why?" when they haven't done what's been assigned or asked of them. When they continue to ignore the Guidelines for Behavior you ensure you have made them clear to this person and that they have been communicated on a regular basis.

You've checked your process every time your problem employee has gone off track. You've tried to make positive corrections each time, to no avail. The Resistance has gotten the best of your employee on a regular basis. Your efforts to affect positive change in your employee through the leadership process have failed.

Here's where the shift takes place. At some point as this poor behavior continues the fault moves from the employee to you, the leader. Why? Because people will continue to exhibit the behavior that is tolerated. If you tolerate a behavior, what you say about the behavior will no longer matter. And this is when we move from accountability to consequence.

When this happens, following the leadership process gives you the justification to implement consequence, which is an unfortunate, but real aspect of leadership. And consequence can mean many things.

Initially, the consequences were simply being held accountable by having to explain their conduct. Everybody goes through this at one point or another, so it's not a big deal. But as the poor behavior continues, the consequences need to become more real and can move to being moved off a project, demoted, or worst of all, terminated.

The point is, because you have followed the process for accountability, you've already done the necessary work to justify the consequences you impose. It's simply a byproduct of following a tried-and-true leadership process and the decision to move to consequence speaks for itself. This is how a leader determines if someone is not a cultural fit to your organization.

Work the Resistance

At this point, you've worked hard at having complete situational awareness at all times. Use your new-found awareness of all things to spot the Resistance and account for it. As with every other challenge you face, when you catch it early enough you will be able to make small, easy adjustments before things get out of hand.

A FINAL NOTE

I T IS MY SINCERE HOPE THAT YOU TRULY MAKE THE PROCESS, Art, and Science of Leadership your own to create massive impact on your life and the lives of those around you. There is nothing more important than leadership in this world. I believe that with every fiber of my being.

When there is no love, a leader will recognize it, find out why, and move people towards love. When there is no patience, a leader will exercise patience in the face of impatience and change the energy of everyone they come in contact with. Leaders move intolerance to tolerance, worthlessness to worthiness, despair to hope, ignorance to understanding, sadness to joy.

You can do all of these things. We all can. But only if we work at it. Only if we care enough to go through the pain of growth in all the aspects of leadership we have discussed throughout this book.

It won't be easy. It will take a discipline and humility (and now you know how to practice both through cold exposure) that is uncommon to the uncommitted. It will take a new mindset. But now you know how to achieve that new mindset. It will take practice to figure out exactly what works for you. But now you know how to practice. You know SMACC. You know cold exposure. You can reflect back and see where you went right and where you went wrong. And now you have that process and its five elements.

As my favorite quote in the world goes, "God will not look you over for medals, degrees, or diplomas, but for scars." Welcome to leadership!

ENDNOTES

[i] Pressfield, Steven. *The War of Art : Break Through the Blocks and Win Your Inner Creative Battles*. 1st ed. North Egremont, MA: Black Irish Entertainment LLC, 2002.

[ii] Dispenza, Dr. Joe. *You Are the Placebo: Making Your Mind Matter*. 2nd ed. Carlsbad, CA: Hay House, 2014.

[iii] Bethune, Sophie. "Stress a Major Health Problem in The U.S., Warns APA." American Psychological Association, October 1, 2007. https://www.apa.org/news/press/releases/2007/10/stress.

[iv] *Rewired: Introduction To Your Brain*. Gaia, 2019. https://www.gaia.com/series/rewired.

[v] Dispenza, Dr. Joe. *Becoming Supernatural: How Common People Are Doing the Uncommon*. 2nd ed. Carlsbad, CA: Hay House, 2019.

[vi] *Rewired: Introduction To Your Brain*. Gaia Network, 2019. https://www.gaia.com/series/rewired.

[vii] Ibid.

[viii] Dispenza, Dr. Joe. *You Are the Placebo: Making Your Mind Matter*. 2nd ed. Carlsbad, CA: Hay House, 2014.

[ix] *Rewired: Introduction To Your Brain*. Gaia Network, 2019. https://www.gaia.com/series/rewired.

[x] Dispenza, Dr. Joe. *Becoming Supernatural: How Common People Are Doing the Uncommon*. 2nd ed. Carlsbad, CA: Hay House, 2019.

[xi] Dispenza, Dr. Joe. *You Are the Placebo: Making Your Mind Matter*. 2nd ed. Carlsbad, CA: Hay House, 2014.

[xii] *Rewired: What Is Change?* Gaia Network, 2019. https://www.gaia.com/series/rewired.

[xiii] Hamilton, David R. "Real vs Imaginary in the Brain and Body." https://drdavidhamilton.com/real-vs-imaginary-in-the-brain-and-body/. David R Hamilton, PhD: Using Science to Inspire, February 19, 2019. https://drdavidhamilton.com/.

[xiv] Dispenza, Dr. Joe. *You Are the Placebo: Making Your Mind Matter*. 2nd ed. Carlsbad, CA: Hay House, 2014.

[xv] Doidge, Norman. *The Brain That Changes Itself: Stories of Personal Triumph from the Frontiers of Brain Science*. 1st ed. New York, NY: Penguin Group, 2007.

[xvi] *Rewired: Introduction To Your Brain*. Gaia Network, 2019. https://www.gaia.com/series/rewired.

[xvii] *Rewired: Demystifying Meditation*. Gaia Network, 2019. https://www.gaia.com/series/rewired.

[xviii] Dispenza, Dr. Joe. *Breaking the Habit of Being Yourself: How to Lose Your Mind and Create a New One*. 1st ed. Carlsbad, CA: Hay House, 2012.

[xix] *Rewired: Survival vs Creation*. Gaia Network, 2019. https://www.gaia.com/series/rewired.

[xx] Dispenza, Dr. Joe. *Becoming Supernatural: How Common People Are Doing the Uncommon*. 2nd ed. Carlsbad, CA: Hay House, 2019.

[xxi] Dispenza, Dr. Joe. *Breaking the Habit of Being Yourself: How to Lose Your Mind and Create a New One*. 1st ed. Carlsbad, CA: Hay House, 2012.

[xxii] Dispenza, Dr. Joe. *You Are the Placebo: Making Your Mind Matter*. 2nd ed. Carlsbad, CA: Hay House, 2014.

[xxiii] *Rewired: Survival vs Creation*. Gaia Network, 2019. https://www.gaia.com/series/rewired.

[xxiv]Dispenza, Dr. Joe. *You Are the Placebo: Making Your Mind Matter.* 2nd ed. Carlsbad, CA: Hay House, 2014.

[xxv]Dispenza, Dr. Joe. *Becoming Supernatural: How Common People Are Doing the Uncommon.* 2nd ed. Carlsbad, CA: Hay House, 2019.

[xxvi] Sarno, John E. *Healing Back Pain: The Mind-Body Connection.* 1st ed. New York, NY: Grand Central Publishing, 1991.

[xxvii] Goldsmith, Marshall, and Mark Reiter. *Triggers: Sparking Positive Change and Making It Last.* 1st ed. New York, NY: Crown Business, 2015.

[xviii] Ibid.

[xxix] Kox, Matthus, Monique Stoffels, Saane P Smeekens, Nens van Alfen, Marc Gomes, Thus M.H. Eusvogels, Maria T.E. Hopman, Johannes G. van der Hoeven, Mihai G. Netea, and Peter Pickkers. "The Influence of Concentration/Meditation on Autonomic Nervous System Activity and the Innate Immune Response: A Case Study." *Psychosomatic Medicine* 74, no. 5 (January 2012): 489–94. https://doi.org/10.1097/PSY.0b013e3182583c6d.

[xxx] Dispenza, Dr. Joe. *You Are the Placebo: Making Your Mind Matter.* 2nd ed. Carlsbad, CA: Hay House, 2014.

[xxxi] Bethune, S., and J. Panlener. "Stress a Major Health Problem in the U.S. Warns APA." *American Psychological Association* 2008 (2007): 92–117.

[xxxii] *Rewired: Introduction To Your Brain.* Gaia Network, 2019. https://www.gaia.com/series/rewired.

[xxxiii] Dispenza, Dr. Joe. *Becoming Supernatural: How Common People Are Doing the Uncommon.* 2nd ed. Carlsbad, CA: Hay House, 2019.

[xxxiv] *Rewired: Introduction To Your Brain.* Gaia Network, 2019. https://www.gaia.com/series/rewired.

[xxxv]Dispenza, Dr. Joe. *Breaking the Habit of Being Yourself: How to Lose Your Mind and Create a New One.* 1st ed. Carlsbad, CA: Hay House, 2012.

[xxxvi] *Rewired: Demystifying Meditation.* Gaia Network, 2019. https://www.gaia.com/series/rewired.

xxxvii Couch, Dick, and William Doyle. *Navy SEALs: Their Untold Story.* 1st ed. New York, NY: Harper Collins, 2014.

xxxviii "SEAL History: Origins of Naval Special Warfare-WWII." Navy SEAL Museum. Accessed May 19, 2020. https://www.navysealmuseum.org/about-navy-seals/seal-history-the-naval-special-warfare-storyseal-history-the-naval-special-warfare-story/seal-history-origins-of-naval-special-warfare-wwii.

xxxix Dispenza, Dr. Joe. *Becoming Supernatural: How Common People Are Doing the Uncommon.* 2nd ed. Carlsbad, CA: Hay House, 2019.

xl Ibid.

xli Dispenza, Dr. Joe. *Breaking the Habit of Being Yourself: How to Lose Your Mind and Create a New One.* 1st ed. Carlsbad, CA: Hay House, 2012.

xlii Ibid.

xliii *Rewired: What Is Change?* Gaia Network, 2019. https://www.gaia.com/series/rewired.

xliv Dispenza, Dr. Joe. *Becoming Supernatural: How Common People Are Doing the Uncommon.* 2nd ed. Carlsbad, CA: Hay House, 2019.

xlv *Rewired: Introduction To Your Brain.* Gaia Network, 2019. https://www.gaia.com/series/rewired.

xlvi Dispenza, Dr. Joe. *You Are the Placebo: Making Your Mind Matter.* 2nd ed. Carlsbad, CA: Hay House, 2014.

xlvii Dispenza, Dr. Joe. *Becoming Supernatural: How Common People Are Doing the Uncommon.* 2nd ed. Carlsbad, CA: Hay House, 2019.

xlviii Ibid.

xlix *Rewired: Introduction To Your Brain.* Gaia Network, 2019. https://www.gaia.com/series/rewired.

l Dispenza, Dr. Joe. *You Are the Placebo: Making Your Mind Matter.* 2nd ed. Carlsbad, CA: Hay House, 2014.

li Dispenza, Dr. Joe. *Becoming Supernatural: How Common People Are Doing the Uncommon.* 2nd ed. Carlsbad, CA: Hay House, 2019.

[lii] *Rewired: Demystifying Meditation.* Gaia Network, 2019. https://www.gaia.com/series/rewired.

[liii] Dispenza, Dr. Joe. *Breaking the Habit of Being Yourself: How to Lose Your Mind and Create a New One.* 1st ed. Carlsbad, CA: Hay House, 2012.

[liv] Kox, Matthus, Monique Stoffels, Saane P Smeekens, Nens van Alfen, Marc Gomes, Thus M.H. Eusvogels, Maria T.E. Hopman, Johannes G. van der Hoeven, Mihai G. Netea, and Peter Pickkers. "The Influence of Concentration/Meditation on Autonomic Nervous System Activity and the Innate Immune Response: A Case Study." *Psychosomatic Medicine* 74, no. 5 (January 2012): 489–94. https://doi.org/10.1097/PSY.0b013e3182583c6d.

[lv] Falls, Jordan. "How to Stimulate Your Vagus Nerve for Better Mental Health." Optimal Living Dynamics, 2020. https://www.optimallivingdynamics.com/blog/how-to-stimulate-your-vagus-nerve-for-better-mental-health-brain-vns-ways-treatment-activate-natural-foods-depression-anxiety-stress-heart-rate-variability-yoga-massage-vagal-tone-dysfunction.

[lvi] Ibid.

[lvii] Cullen, Susan. "Why Leadership Training Is Essential in Your Organization." Quantum Learning Solutions, Inc, October 2, 2017. https://www.quantumlearn.com/blog/why-leadership-training-is-essential-in-your-organization.

[lviii] Witt, David. "The High Cost of Doing Nothing: Quantifying the Impact of Leadership on the Bottom Line." The Ken Blanchard Companies, December 10, 2009. https://leaderchat.org/2009/12/10/leadership-development-the-high-cost-of-doing-nothing-understanding-the-financial-impact/.

[lix] Ibid.

[lx] Ibid.

[lxi] Ibid.

[lxii] Duhigg, Charles. *Smarter Faster Better.* 1st ed. New York, NY: Random House, 2016.

lxiii Ibid.

lxiv Ibid.

lxv Ibid.

lxvi Ibid.

lxvii Thompson, Leigh. "How to Neutralize a Meeting Tyrant." Fortune, February 11, 2013. http://fortune.com/2013/02/11/how-to-neutralize-a-meeting-tyrant/.

lxviii Duhigg, Charles. *Smarter Faster Better*. 1st ed. New York, NY: Random House, 2016.

lxix *Rewired: Introduction To Your Brain*. Gaia Network, 2019. https://www.gaia.com/series/rewired.

lxx Ibid.

lxxi Dispenza, Dr. Joe. *Becoming Supernatural: How Common People Are Doing the Uncommon*. 2nd ed. Carlsbad, CA: Hay House, 2019.

lxxii Doidge, Norman. *The Brain That Changes Itself: Stories of Personal Triumph from the Frontiers of Brain Science*. 1st ed. New York, NY: Penguin Group, 2007.

lxxiii *Rewired: Introduction To Your Brain*. Gaia Network, 2019. https://www.gaia.com/series/rewired.

lxxiv Ibid.

lxxv Dispenza, Dr. Joe. *You Are the Placebo: Making Your Mind Matter*. 2nd ed. Carlsbad, CA: Hay House, 2014.

lxxvi Bethune, S., and J. Panlener. "Stress a Major Health Problem in the U.S. Warns APA." *American Psychological Association* 2008 (2007): 92–117.

lxxvii Dispenza, Dr. Joe. *Breaking the Habit of Being Yourself: How to Lose Your Mind and Create a New One*. 1st ed. Carlsbad, CA: Hay House, 2012.

lxxviii Dispenza, Dr. Joe. *Becoming Supernatural: How Common People Are Doing the Uncommon*. 2nd ed. Carlsbad, CA: Hay House, 2019.

lxxix Dispenza, Dr. Joe. *You Are the Placebo: Making Your Mind Matter*. 2nd ed. Carlsbad, CA: Hay House, 2014.

[lxxx] Pressfield, Steven. *The War of Art : Break Through the Blocks and Win Your Inner Creative Battles*. 1st ed. North Egremont, MA: Black Irish Entertainment LLC, 2002.

Made in the USA
Columbia, SC
08 July 2020